UNDERSTANDING
YOUR HORSE

UNDERSTANDING YOUR HORSE

How to Overcome Common Behaviour Problems

Lesley Bayley &
Richard Maxwell

DAVID & CHARLES

A DAVID & CHARLES BOOK

Photographs courtesy of *Your Horse* magazine and Angus Murray

First published in the UK in 1996
Copyright © Lesley Bayley & Richard Maxwell 1996
Lesley Bayley & Richard Maxwell have asserted their right to be
identified as authors of this work in accordance with the Copyright,
Designs and Patents Act, 1988.

A catalogue record for this book is available from the British Library.

ISBN 0 7153 0346 5

Design by Visual Image
and printed in Italy by Milanostampa SpA
for David & Charles
Brunel House   Newton Abbot   Devon

CONTENTS

INTRODUCING THE HORSE

*A good horseman hears his horse talking to him,
a great horseman can hear the horse whisper,
but bad horsemen cannot even hear the horse screaming.*

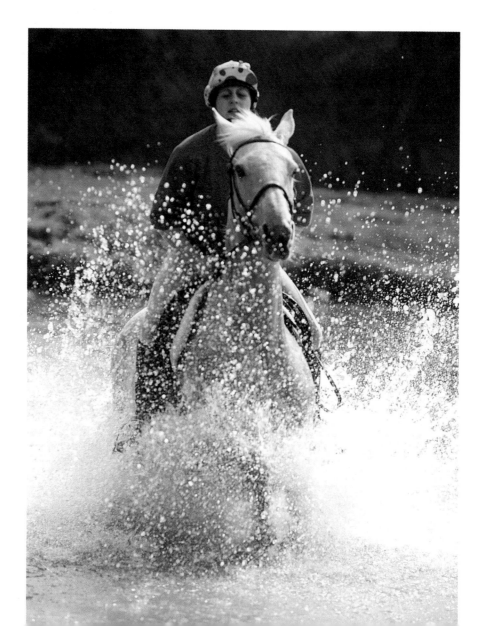

For a horse in pain or distress, the fact that so many people fall into the last category as described in this saying, only serves to heighten his plight. It is very often the case that horses are misunderstood and labelled as difficult when in fact they are suffering. For example, it is relatively common for a horse to trap a nerve or put a neck vertebra out, and his only way of telling us that he is in pain is to demonstrate his problem in the way he moves or behaves.

Just as humans have different pain thresholds, so it is with horses; thus some will put up with incredible discomfort for long periods, whilst others will let you know immediately anything is slightly wrong. The problem is that many people are unable to recognise the signs: they are deaf to their horse, even when he is 'screaming' as loud as he can. Take the real-life example of a horse that bucked on landing every time he jumped. This particular horse really did not want to go forwards – even when he jumped. When he had no other choice but to jump a fence he did so as quickly as possible, and then bucked like mad on the landing side. His young owner thought this was all rather impressive and good fun; in reality, the horse was suffering a great deal of pain in his back. This was something the owner found difficult to cope with, however, largely because she had been taught, as are many people, that when a horse misbehaves it has to be shown that such behaviour is not acceptable. This sort of approach is highly superficial because it means that no one bothers to look for the real cause of the problem: the horse's cry for help is not simply ignored, it isn't even heard.

The way in which most of us handle horses is based upon customary procedure handed down from generation to generation, most of which we accept without question as 'normal' practice. But why not challenge this norm? For example, when 'breaking' a horse, why do we always get him used to the saddle before we put a rider on board? Consider this formula for a change, that if a horse respects his handler and is used to him touching him all over, then he might be happier to accept the *handler* on his back in the first instance, rather than the strange element of the saddle? Just because a certain method is accepted practice does not mean that it is the most effective or the right way of doing things. Sometimes practices have developed with very little thought for the unfortunate horse on the receiving end of our training. All too often we fail to question what we are doing, and more significantly, we don't notice what the horse is telling us.

Horsemen need not remain deaf to their horses, however, and it is perfectly possible to develop the skills, knowledge and sensitivity required to be able to at least hear your horse speak.

Prey Animals and Predators

One fundamental point which must be understood is that horses have always been identified as prey animals, and humans as predators. This has far-reaching effects on the way our horses behave, and thousands

THINK LIKE A HORSE

To win a horse's confidence we have to learn to behave in a manner which is less like a predator: this means we must think more like a prey animal, which in this case means thinking more like a horse. Once a person crosses this line and starts to appreciate the horse's point of view, then progress can be made, not only in solving difficult situations but also in preventing further problems arising. So as to hear your horse you must open your mind and start questioning what is happening in his. Furthermore, what you learn from thinking like a horse can be applied not just to your own horses, but also to any others you may deal with in the future.

Achieving a true partnership with a horse takes time, patience and an open mind

Treat the horse as a horse: it does not have human attributes, but is an animal with thousands of years of instinctive behaviour programmed into it.

Take the opportunity to introduce your young horse to the sights he'll meet in future such as dogs, cyclists and walkers

It is important to realise that the horse *does* communicate with you, not just through his voice, but more importantly by his body language and behaviour – and you can learn to recognise and understand his language.

of years of domestication have not eradicated this behaviour syndrome from the equine make-up: horses still react according to their basic instincts. Thus as prey animals they must be constantly on the alert for danger, and ready to react accordingly. Being naturally timid, they prefer to gallop away if something scares them, although if trapped and forced to fight they will kick, bite, buck and rear: they will do whatever is necessary to dislodge the predator if it is on their back, or injure it if it is on the ground.

The horse's eyes are set on the side of his head so he has virtual 360° vision; his only blind spots are immediately in front of and behind him. When grazing he can see predators which are trying to creep up on him, and once he spots danger his stance will alert the other members of the herd: his whole body tenses, his head is held high, his tail raised, his eyes focus on whatever it is that worries him and he is ready to flee. Most riders have known their horses take this stance, often because of something in the far distance which is invisible to the human eye.

The horse's visual faculties may cause him to behave in ways which can be misunderstood by humans. For instance, if his head is held high he cannot see the ground in front of him, so if he wants to look at something down there he will naturally want to lower his head and neck in order to do so. If he is not allowed to do this he may try tilting his head so that he can focus on the object; and if he still cannot see he may resort to moving sideways to improve his view. This action is known as shying, and the next time your horse does this, consider whether you forced him into it. Perhaps you could have avoided the problem by letting him drop his head to have a good look at the object: and if he shied in order to see the object properly, and you told him off, what conclusion will he draw? He will just have learned to associate whatever he couldn't see with a reprimand, and so will make sure he avoids it in future!

Bearing in mind that horses are not naturally bold, it is amazing that they can be taught to overcome their natural instincts in so many different ways: to jump over or off fences when they cannot see the landing side, to jump into water or from light into dark, to walk calmly past huge lorries or rattling tractors, to stand in a confined space and be transported around our motorways, stay 'trapped' in a stable for long periods, and so on.

Just why will they do this? In equine society there is a leader: one horse which is the boss, and which the others respect and obey. If as a human you can prove to your horse that you are the leader, then he will bow to your judgement. For most humans, achieving this position is difficult, especially since we often unwittingly behave instinctively in the manner of a predator. Take the situation in the wild where a predator approaches a watering hole: he can march up to it and drink, for he fears nothing. A prey animal, however, first has to check if it is safe to drink, so his approach to the watering hole will be much more circuitous: he will stop, start, look out for danger, possibly retreat, only advance again once it is safe. Now consider the manner in which we often go to catch a horse: imagine a field of two-year-olds which have had little contact with humans since they were weaned from their dams. We march straight up to a youngster, and are annoyed when he decides to clear off! But he is only acting instinctively: your behaviour is indicating that you are a predator, and the prey animal's natural reaction is to run off. From the horse's point of view his reaction is perfectly logical.

If, however, you were to indicate to the horse that you were not a predator you would have more success, and you can do that by acting more like a prey animal. Remember how the prey animal has to take two steps forward and one back in order to reach the watering hole? Use this advance-and-retreat method to approach a horse, and you will give him the chance to decide whether you are a threat or not.

All horses have their own 'personal space', and are most particular

NATURAL VERSUS DOMESTICATED

In a wild state horses move round in small herds, covering several miles each day in their search for food and water. However, many domesticated horses are shut in a stable and are lucky to have an hour's ridden exercise per day; if they are turned out, it is into a restricted area – even a twenty-acre (8ha) field is small when you consider that horses in the wild roam huge tracts of land – and they are often overfed. Some are unfortunate enough to have to live alone, too, unlike wild horses which rarely live in solitude. So it is not surprising that problems develop.

High jinks in the field: all domesticated horses need their own time, at liberty, just to be a horse

Understand that your horse can read your body language, even though you may not even be aware that you are sending any signals.

as to whom they will allow into this area. Some horses are especially wary, and it is impossible to approach within twenty feet of them before they become jittery and will move away; others are happy to let you right into their world, and so are easy to catch. They will apply this selectivity to other horses as well as humans. Watch a group of horses out in a field and you will be able to work out who is favoured and who isn't. Good friends will graze happily side by side and will probably combine forces to see off any unwelcome intruders; my mare is quite happy to let one particular gelding within ten feet of her, but no one else is allowed this privilege under any circumstances. She is fussy about who catches her as well: those who are noisy, bossy and abrupt have no chance; but those who are quiet, firm and confident are successful, even if sometimes they have to adopt the advance-and-retreat method for five minutes.

Ways of Communication

Horses have a very good communications system, and convey information about all kinds of things using their voice and body language. Neighs, nickers, squeals and snorts carry a number of vocal messages, whilst the outline of the horse's body reveals its emotional state. The way in which the tail, mouth, nose, ears and legs are used indicates the horse's feelings, and it is by recognising these pointers that we can start to understand a horse's feelings and state of mind.

Whilst we can learn a great deal from appreciating a horse's body language, it can understand ours already! For example, when a person is tense this is usually manifested in stiff, jerky movements which the horse instantly recognises as an indication that something is amiss. If he sees his human as the leader, and perceives that the leader is evidently worried, his own anxiety will be heightened – and it is the reason why frightened riders cannot get horses to jump over tiny fences.

Horses learn to comprehend a few of our words – they halt, walk on, trot and so on, on command – but we, with our supposedly superior intelligence, make little effort to learn their language. For many, many years equines have been communicating in universal terms, so that a horse from the English countryside could be put in Russia and all the horses would be able to understand each other. However, we humans could not pass such a language test!

The world over, a horse is a horse: not for them the sort of snobbery which we impose! Thus a Thoroughbred will happily converse with a Shetland even though its owners might be wincing! Equine language embraces all breeds, colours and types – and the only barriers to riders and owners understanding horses are the ones we impose ourselves. So, cast away your pride and ego and embark on an incredible journey.

You will see from this brief overview that owning, training and riding a horse is a complex, demanding business. It places great demands on us, mentally, emotionally and physically. It requires us to put ourselves in the place of another living being and is a long-term commitment; but the rewards are priceless.

Invest time in your horse: spend as much time as you can with him, enjoy him in and out of the saddle, take the trouble to watch him at liberty, and study his behaviour so that you can piece together the many different facets which make up the whole picture of his individual character.

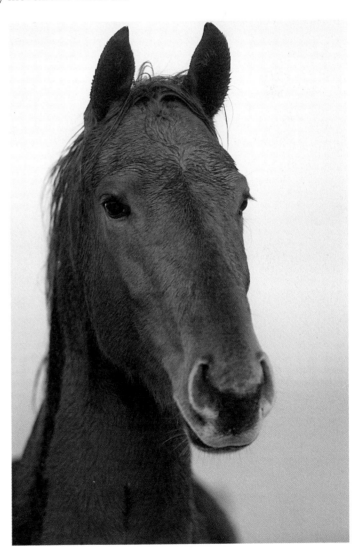

Horses have very good eyesight, and often react to things their riders or handlers cannot see

LINES OF
COMMUNICATION

*Non-horsey people – and indeed many horsey ones!
– find it difficult to 'read' a horse: they fail even to see, let alone interpret
the expression on his face, the way his ears and eyes tell stories, the tension
or relaxation in his body and the clues to his state of mind
as exhibited by his tail position. Indeed, even the horse's vocal calls
are ignored or misunderstood.*

To achieve a true partnership with your horse it is essential to learn to communicate with him: to learn to listen, to see, to understand. Just as humans can give away their real feelings without meaning to, so horses, through their body language and their voices, can clearly indicate to us their emotional state. Eighty per cent of the horse's communication is non-verbal; but first let us look at the calls and noises he makes and how to distinguish each type.

Take time to watch horses at liberty in their fields, and so learn how equine society operates. You will see plenty of 'play' fights, particularly amongst youngsters. If there is a serious dispute you will see threats, made in varying degrees of seriousness, before any physical contact is made

Vocal Expressions
Neighing

The neigh is the general recognition or contact call. Horses have individual voices so can recognise their friends and companions by their neigh just as we can recognise a friend's voice on the telephone. We may not have spoken to someone for months but we can still recognise their voice, and horses are the same. A mare of mine was in a different yard for six months and became good friends with a gelding. We then moved yards, but some three months later met the gelding and his owner at a show. Just as we humans called to each other, the horses also started a noisy exchange of neighs across the collecting ring, changing to nickers as they came closer together.

Think about the occasions your horse neighs: perhaps when he is taken into a stable block and there are no other horses; when you unload at a show; if a friend is taken out of sight. Notice, too, how a horse tends to raise his head when neighing in order to make best use of the throat, just as a singer adopts a particular posture when trying to reach the high notes.

Listen to the character and pitch of the neigh: the call of an excited stallion is quite different to that for example of an animal which is upset, such as a mare or foal which have lost sight of each other.

Having a partnership with your horse whereby he will trust you at all times is satisfying – and can also be life-saving. If there is a fire you may need to get him out of the stable by placing a blindfold over his head, and if he is happy for you to do this it will save vital seconds

Nickering

A horse's nicker is a lower and shorter sound than a neigh, the most delightful surely being that of a mare speaking to her foal – the sound is very soft and maternal. Nickers are used between equine friends, and to greet human friends, too; and the stallion has a very particular courtship nicker in his vocabulary.

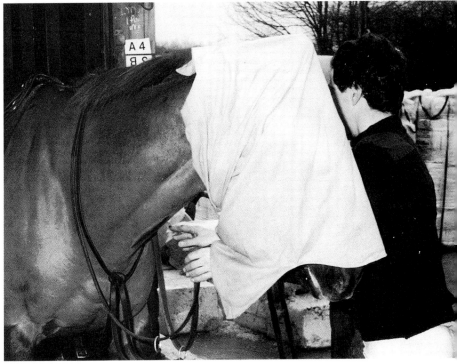

Squealing

The squeal is a familiar sound, particularly if you own a flirty mare – in the company of geldings you'll probably hear a great deal of squealing, often accompanied by a stamping forefoot. A meeting between strangers – male or female – can result in similar reaction. Squealing is also a significant part of the courtship procedure between a mare and stallion, indicating excitement.

Squealing may be used as a warning, and to show resentment; for example, a mare with a foal at foot will squeal at another mare to keep her away from the foal. She will not, however, use a squeal in isolation but will accompany it with flattened ears, swinging her rump to the 'intruder' mare.

This mare's body language is quite clear, and the older youngster knows that he had better keep out of the way

Snorting

Most riders will have experienced their horses snorting at a 'monster', whether this is in the form of a road sign, a person with an umbrella or some other strange sight. Some horses are genuinely alarmed, others are just full of high spirits and like to play at being worried, producing horrified snorts for extra effect. The sight and smell of pigs often causes much of this sort of behaviour. In the wild, stallions will snort when challenging each other. Whatever the circumstance, the horse usually adopts a high head and tail carriage as well, and is very much on its toes – ready to flee if the 'monster' is genuinely dangerous.

Grunting

Grunts and groans may also be heard: for example, some horses grunt if making a great effort (perhaps jumping). A mare foaling will often grunt, as may a horse in pain from colic, or when he is getting up.

Body Language

Next we will look at the various parts of the horse's body and investigate how they convey certain messages; however, remember that the biggest clue as to how the horse is feeling is provided by his overall appearance. For example, a horse turned out at liberty which is scared by something reacts quite distinctively, and the whole of its body and the way in which it moves presents a picture of excitement: the neck is arched, the head and tail are held high, the ears are pricked, all the muscles seem to stand out and the steps are elevated. Other horses seeing this display will also become excited, and in the wild this 'startle' posture would alert other members of the herd to danger.

A dozing or sick horse, on the other hand, presents a completely different picture: the head and neck are lowered, the tail carriage is low, a hindleg may be rested and there will be no sign of excitement at all in its outline.

Stallions and mares adopt certain postures during their courtship procedures as well as making use of smell and touch.

The Tail

Whilst a high tail carriage indicates that a horse is excited, a clamped-down tail shows fear and submission. Frightened or anxious horses also pass droppings more frequently; extreme anxiety may even result in diarrhoea. Recently I collected a young horse for a friend. The youngster had travelled in lorries on two previous occasions without any bad experiences, and was happy to go into my lorry after five minutes of sniffing the ramp and being allowed to proceed at his own pace. However, he did four small piles of droppings in that short time!

Observe your horse and make a point of noticing how the tail is used: for example, when greeting his friends it will be slightly higher than normal; when he is sleepy his tail carriage will be low – but nothing like the 'tucked-under' look that accompanies a horse which is afraid. An apprehensive horse will hold his tail so that the dock shows through the hair.

The Ears

The horse has several pairs of muscles in each ear, so there is tremendous scope for movement. When he is startled or has seen something in the distance both ears will be forward and pricked. One ear back and one forward means his attention is split, whilst droopy ears show a lack of attention. Submission may be shown by the

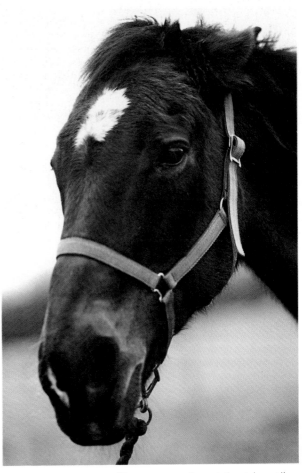

The message here is 'watch out!' for this horse is unhappy about something!

ears being back or partially back, and the latter position also indicates doziness. Fearful horses have their ears back, whilst the ears flat back denotes fear and anger. As some ear positions may mean two contrasting things (ears partially back, for example), then the other signals the horse is emitting have to be considered.

The Mouth

One of the most obvious signals is that made by foals who will open and close the mouth in a series of snapping movements with the lips drawn back and the teeth exposed. This shows other horses that they are submissive; foals may also behave like this towards humans or to any other big objects. As they grow older they will cease to react in this way, but the age at which this occurs depends on the individual's boldness.

The other distinctive mouth signal that most people will have witnessed is the Flehmen posture, when the nose is held high and the top lip is curled upwards exposing the teeth. Stallions use this a great deal when smelling the urine of a mare in season, but other horses also use it in a non-sexual way, if they taste or smell something unexpected.

Dozing horses will often have a relaxed, droopy bottom lip, while anxious, upset or confused animals will have a tense, tight mouth.

Horses indulging in mutual grooming will elongate the top lip and use it like a probe, as they do when scratching about in a feed bucket or someone's pockets for food.

When meeting adult horses, foals know that there are certain ways of behaving. The older horse looks fairly sleepy at this moment but the foal will be ready to 'mouth' and show he is submissive

Head and Neck Movements

Watching horses at grass is a very good way to observe different types of behaviour and communication. Friends may nudge each other as a prelude to grooming, in the same way that horses often nudge their owners when seeking attention. These movements are fairly slow and gentle, whereas a thrust with the head is more aggressive and generally accompanied with ears flattened and mouth open in a threat to bite. Such a gesture might be used by a horse which does not want you to enter his stable.

Horses that are startled may jerk their head back; and they will shake it vigorously to get rid of anything annoying, be it a fly or a bit. A horse may also swing his head and neck away, for example if he is headshy.

Sometimes a horse is seen to adopt a low neck carriage with head and neck outstretched and snaking his head from side to side. Stallions adopt this position, together with a high leg movement, when

rounding up their mares. A gelding of mine used it when he was thoroughly fed up with the activities of his field mate.

Leg Movements

Horses meeting for the first time often squeal and strike out with a foreleg; this reaction is intended as a warning not to be too familiar.

Pawing is the horse's way of investigating things; thus a young foal being loaded for the first time will test the ramp of the lorry by pawing and sniffing at it. Pawing also has a more practical use, that of breaking the ice on a water supply and clearing snow away from grazing. It may also indicate frustration and anger.

The coloured horse is the dominant one in this field, and his head thrusts are enough to send the other horse on its way

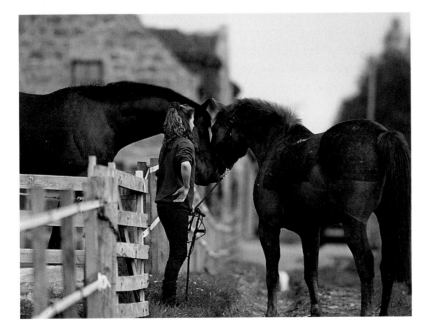

Introducing a new horse into an established group needs to be done sensibly. Squeals and lashing out with a foreleg often accompany such meetings

Mares will admonish their offspring, and threats usually suffice

Understanding Horse Behaviour

Have you ever asked yourself why all horses are initially suspicious of going into water, or onto any new or untested surface? Why is it that they dislike shadows on roads, or white line markings, or hollow-sounding bridges? And if you fall off, how come your horse makes such tremendous efforts to avoid stepping on you? Why don't horses like hoses on the floor or anything around their feet?

In the wild the horse survives by running away, and in order to do this his feet and legs must be sound. If they are not, then his life is in danger; this is why foals are on their feet within an hour of birth. His primary concern, therefore, is to avoid risking his feet and limbs by walking into anything untested. If, however, he sees the other herd members walking on it safely, then he will invariably follow. This is why horses will follow the lead of others into water, over fences, into lorries and so on. And if their rider, who should also be their leader, is happy to walk into the water first, then again the horse will generally follow.

For one whose main defence is flight, the horse's worst scenario must be confinement, with no way of escaping his enemies. And even though domesticated horses have learned to accept confinement in stables, they still prefer to be free: given the choice, they will generally stand out in all weathers rather than use nearby shelters. It is essential to understand that horses are claustrophobic, for this affects their attitude to stabling and being transported in lorries and trailers. It is primarily for our convenience that we keep our horses stabled, and it is for our enjoyment that we transport them around to shows. But if we are going to do this, the least we can do is provide them with a light, airy, spacious stable and trailer, as well as ensuring they are turned out to grass for as long as possible each day to play and relax.

Something else which goes against the grain for horses is being restrained: again, the reason is their instinctive programming, their need to be able to flee from danger. Yet domesticated horses do allow themselves to be restrained. One of the first lessons my young foal learned was to respect the halter. Richard Maxwell spent twenty minutes with him, using a very kind, low-key method; basically he let the youngster make up his own mind to submit to pressure on the halter, waiting until he stepped forwards towards the pressure of his own volition. When the colt did this the pressure was released, and he was praised and rewarded with a rub on the head. If this lesson takes place when the foal is just a couple of months old it will stay with him for life, making things as diverse as learning to be tied up and loading into a lorry much easier.

Communication also includes touch: your partnership with your horse should include plenty of rewards in the form of pats. Horses can usually sense whether you are pleased with them or not

Handling the Horse in his own Language

When handling horses you need to establish that you are the dominant member of the herd, although there is little value in using force to do this as the horse does not fully appreciate this method: whilst he may succumb initially there will come a point when he will pit his strength against yours, and in such a confrontation it is inevitable that the human will lose. What the horse does react to, though, is his own language; so by using equine body language you can establish that you are the dominant force in the herd.

We have to counteract the superior strength of horses with our intellect: by using psychology we can communicate with the horse at a much deeper level, and the beauty is that every horse will understand us.

Take your body language: if you adopt an aggressive stance by making yourself physically big – simply by looking up, keeping eye contact with the horse and holding out your arms to give the impression of being bigger than you are – then the horse will read this signal and look upon you as being the aggressor, and you will be treated with respect. Try this out in the field and see how the animals react.

If, however, you avoid eye contact, bow your head and round your shoulders, you are adopting a passive stance (in the eyes of the horse) and are therefore non-aggressive. Bear in mind that each group of horses will have a 'pecking' order, with some horses being more dominant and more bullying than others.

Horses have their own physical space – usually about twenty feet in diameter around them – into which you have to be invited. Their friends in the group will be allowed access

Being aware of your posture and the signals you are emitting is vital when handling horses, and particularly those which may take advantage of a less-than-confident handler. You need to act and look confident even if you are feeling unsure, and whatever you do, never be hesitant, because you will only promote a feeling of suspicion from the horse. For example, if you fail to ride positively towards a fence, your uncertainty will be transmitted to the horse which will then stop – after all, if you are not confident about jumping (and you know what's on the landing side), why should the horse have the confidence for both of you?

Remember that the horse reacts to you: the situation should not arise where you react to the horse, and if this does happen then it is the horse that has taken control. This applies when both handling and riding horses. Be confident: using eye contact and your body language demand the horse's attention. Build his confidence in you by being decisive but whilst moving slowly and deliberately in your handling of him. Be patient but firm, remembering that your voice can be a powerful tool; that you can soothe, calm, reprimand or motivate a horse by the tone of your voice alone.

SUMMARY

This horse has whipped around rather than jump the fence as requested; her whole outline reflects the tenseness of the situation

- Spend time watching horses at liberty so that you can understand their social hierarchy better, and how they use their language (both verbal and non-verbal) to communicate with each other.

- Always consider your horse's basic instincts: we think of picking out his feet as a very simple task, yet it is a huge step for him to surrender his means of flight, and in so doing he is showing the remarkable degree to which he puts his trust in you; so never undervalue your horse's good will or become complacent about it, and about all he does for you.

- Be confident around horses: learn how to use your body language so that you can convey the correct message to your horse.

- Take care not to give your horse the impression that you are submissive: you can be passive, but if you are submissive some horses will take advantage of you and will completely take over the situation. This will result is many problems for you: remember, *you* have to act as the dominant member of the herd.

- The equine equivalent of personality consists of three ingredients: innate characteristics, 'learned' behaviour, and spirit. The so-called innate characteristics derive from the horse's genetic make-up; his 'learned' behaviour comes from the influence of a) his dam, b) the herd, c) his environment, d) humans; and spirit is the amount of energy he puts into things. Make sure that you buy a horse with a personality that is compatible with yours: so many people buy horses with too much spirit and thus overhorse themselves.

Youngsters, and colts in particular, will explore with their mouths. However, it is a fine line between allowing them this natural activity, which will probably include a little nipping, and the serious problem of biting

THE EFFECTS OF PAIN

*Horses are amazingly tolerant creatures, often adapting
their way of going to accommodate discomfort –
as, for example, that caused by a poorly fitting saddle.
However, when discomfort turns to pain the horse's tolerance
threshold may be breached…and
his only way of letting his rider and owner know
he is hurting could be through serious misbehaviour.*

When horses are sent to Richard Maxwell's yard it is often because their owners have failed to resolve their problems themselves; they have tried all the methods they know but still their horses persist in 'misbehaving'. For the horses, Max represents their last chance, and if he cannot succeed, then humane destruction is often the next step. The sad fact is that the majority of the horses he is asked to sort out are in pain or discomfort, and the only way they can communicate to their owners that something is wrong is by behaving badly. Initially the signal which a horse sends out indicating that something is amiss may be very subtle, and may not be recognised as such by the owner. As the pain or discomfort increases, however, so the horse's 'conversation' becomes more violent; thus an initial reluctance to move forwards may develop into nappiness, and may ultimately progress to a serious demonstration of rearing.

◀ There has to be a reason for your horse resisting your requests, and the majority of 'problem' cases which find themselves in Max's yard are in pain to some degree. Each horse has its individual pain threshold: some may be suffering agony, but their owners may not even know

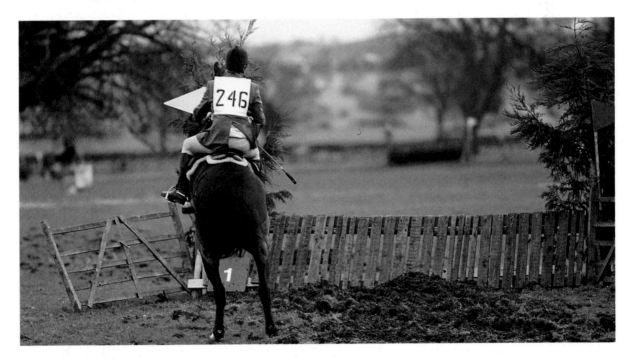

Unfortunately, equitation as taught to many of us instils in us the conviction that the horse must do as he is told. So if he does not behave as we expect him to, then the first thing we do is to punish him, insisting that he obeys us by employing the various means of coercion at our disposal, namely the whip and spurs.

What we should do, however, as owners, riders and handlers, is to stop and think a little more. If a horse which is normally tractable suddenly starts to be resistant, there has to be a reason, and we ought to try and establish the cause of the problem before we start laying down the law. After all, if we were ill we would not be very impressed with a doctor who administered treatment without even bothering to question us about our symptoms. Yet in effect that is just what we do

Rearing could be because of excitement, for example in a competition situation, or it could be caused by pain

with our horses: we hand out a remedy without even considering the reasons that cause the misdemeanour.

Certainly there are horses which do misbehave simply because they know they can get the better of a particular rider; if this is the case with you and your horse then it is up to you either to improve your riding and ensure you are of a suitable standard to cope, or to acknowledge that you have over-horsed yourself, in which case you should find the animal a more suitable home and replace it with one better suited to your abilities. Ultimately the responsibility for a horse's health and daily welfare lies with its owner; there is no escaping this fact and, as owners, we must acknowledge this and act upon it: the horse cannot change its situation, but we can, and should, whatever the reason. and as regards those horses in pain or discomfort which are doing their best to tell us, their owners/handlers, or their trouble, again it is our responsibility to learn how to interpret their appearance and understand what they are trying to say.

The level of pain a horse can withstand varies according to each individual, just as it does with people, and the degrees of pain range from mild discomfort and tension to acute distress. How much a horse reacts depends on individual tolerance and pain threshold. For example you may own a horse which is suffering relatively mild

Why is this horse playing up? Is it because he doesn't want to leave his friends, or because he is genuinely frightened of what he is being asked to do? Is he confused about what is being asked of him? Or is he hurting, or being plain naughty? Getting to the root of a problem is not easy, but at least if you can eliminate the common cause, which is pain, you're off to a good start

discomfort but is very sensitive, so he may in fact display the same symptoms as a less demonstrative horse which is going through absolute hell.

Getting to know your horse really well is excellent advice in regard to all aspects of horse management, but is particularly apt for behavioural problems. Keeping a diary helps, too: often the first signs of trouble are only small, and as isolated incidents they may not mean very much; but when pieced together they show how circumstances develop. Making notes of your horse's daily life means you can look back over the days or weeks and see the whole picture. Writing things down also ensures that you become more observant and start to think more about what is happening.

So what do you include in your horse's daily diary? Note down any reactions which are out of the ordinary, when he is being ridden, when he is turned out or caught, when he is being tacked up or groomed and so on. It could be that he starts to pull a face when you appear with the saddle, or is heavier on one rein when schooling, or hangs around the field gate instead of going off with his friends, or maybe he doesn't eat his feed as quickly. If you notice anything adverse then you should carry out other checks to satisfy yourself that he is not incubating an illness: for instance, if he is off his feed then check his temperature, the also the colour of his membranes, the amount he is drinking, the amount and colour of his droppings. Becoming more observant means that you can identify the symptoms of possible illness at an early stage and seek veterinary help, if needs be, sooner rather than later.

Always ensure that you check the horse's legs before and after he has worked. When you pick out his feet, it takes only a little extra effort to feel for heat or bumps in the legs as well. Check his glands as you put on the bridle or headcollar, and take a look at the inside of his nostrils as you do up the bridle noseband. Just a little thought and a few extra seconds and you can learn so much more about your animal.

Such daily observations will build up a whole picture of your horse's normal behaviour, so that if he tells you something is wrong by 'whispering' to you, you will understand and can help him straightaway, and he won't have to wait until his condition is so bad that he is screaming at you in pain.

Recognising the Symptoms of Pain

Naturally there may be other reasons why the horse behaves in the ways outlined above, but it is your responsibility to establish whether it is pain or not. If you know without doubt that the cause is not pain, then you are justified in using more persuasive methods (see Chapters 6 and 7 for methods which understand the horse's psychology, rather than methods which make little sense to him).

One of the training tenets we are all taught is that repetition is necessary for the horse to understand what you want. This assumption

KEEP AN OPEN MIND

In order to understand your horse it is important to free yourself of any restrictions imposed by your previous equestrian education. For instance, don't accept any judgement conferred on a horse without questioning its validity: some people are so entrenched in their own, blinkered way of thinking that they will not even consider other ideas. So if you are told that a horse *always* tries to bite you when he is tacked up, or that a horse habitually puts his head in the air when you try to bridle him, *don't* just accept the explanation that 'it's just him'. Remember: there is always a reason, and it's up to *you* to identify it.

RECOGNISING THE SYMPTOMS OF PAIN

The ways in which a horse may tell you that he is in pain or suffering discomfort are many and varied:

- Pulling faces when you appear with the tack
- Refusing to open his mouth for the bit to be put in
- Raising his head so the bridle cannot be put on easily
- Moving to the back of the stable when you come in with the tack
- Dipping his back when the saddle is put on
- Kicking out or biting when the saddle is put on or the girth is tightened
- Refusing to stand still when you are trying to mount
- Moving off as soon as you mount
- Dipping his back or appearing to collapse when you mount
- Refusing to go forwards
- Refusing to move at all
- Running backwards
- Rearing
- Bucking
- Napping
- Shying
- Refusing to stretch his neck forwards

- Going along with his head high in the air, a hollow back and trailing hindquarters
- Rushing on the flat and over fences
- Refusing to take the rein forwards
- Running through the rein (when he appears to ignore the bit completely and bears down on the rider's hands)
- Pulling, running off or bolting
- 'Freaking out' during a ridden session
- Being behind the bit
- Not wanting to jump, shown by nappiness and refusing to go near a fence, or by approaching a fence at great speed, throwing himself over and then rushing off on the landing side
- Refusing at a fence (running out tends to be a rider problem)
- Bucking on landing after a fence
- Taking short strides (propping) before take-off at a fence
- Cat-jumping a fence, rather than taking it on with flowing style
- Shortening the stride, generally an indication of sore feet
- Moving in a 'crabby' way, for example round corners or on circles
- Lack of freedom in the paces
- Becoming disunited in canter

should be qualified, however: if the lesson you are repeating is within the horse's capabilities and makes sense to him, then it is perfectly legitimate; but if the repetition involves an unacceptable status quo – for example, the horse is in pain, but is being roughly punished for saying so – then the effect on him is bound to be extremely negative. Thus in order for a horse to progress in his learning we must also take into account his natural instincts; for example he will naturally be suspicious and unwilling to go into a dark, confined space such as a trailer. Equine psychology is a fascinating subject and once you start to understand it, it becomes increasingly obvious how closely the great variety of equine problems are related, and how easy it is to address them without causing further stress to the horse.

Learning Through Experience

Throughout a horse's training it is important to appreciate how he sees, hears and thinks, and how we can use this to build a partnership with him. As already mentioned in Chapter 2, we must first establish ourselves as the herd leader in his eyes; we can often then manoeuvre a

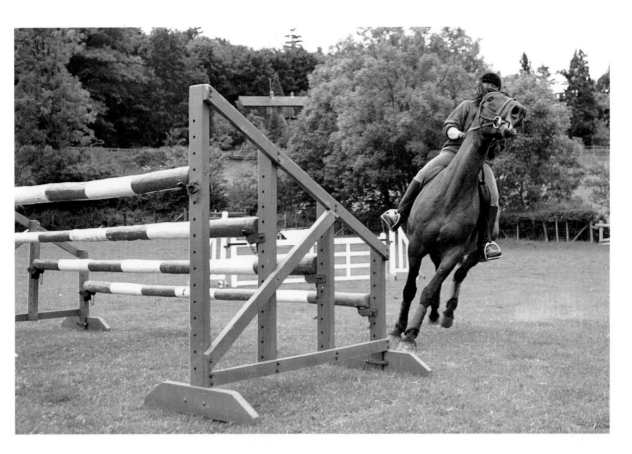

situation so that the horse learns and makes the right decisions for himself: for example, he decides it is better *not* to rear than to rear (see case history of rearer). When a horse has made a decision *for himself*, then he will be committed to it; but if we try to make the decision for him by forcing him to behave, then he will not feel committed to it and will almost certainly misbehave again.

We all know that learning through our own experience is much more successful in driving something home: 'secondhand' experience – being *told* that it is good or bad for us – simply doesn't have the same effect. Naturally we are all curious about many aspects of life, but once we have acquired the personal experience of something bad, such as burning our fingers on a match, we are not so keen to repeat it.

Horses learn from experience, too. For instance when starting a horse, Max always lets it get used to the feel of a saddle unrestrained. In a round pen, for safety's sake, it is allowed to move off and to buck and leap about entirely at will with this strange piece of equipment on its back: in other words, it is allowed to follow its instincts – namely to get this object off. By doing this, the horse will learn through its own experience that this saddle will not harm it, but it will not be dislodged, either. Once they have experienced this, horses then accept the saddle of their own volition, and Max feels that if they are not allowed this experience there is always the likelihood that they will follow their instincts at some later stage.

Riders must be honest with themselves if they are to understand their horses. This horse may have run out because in its experience jumping results in pain – or it may have run out because the rider is not truly committed to jumping a fence of this size

Recognising Stress

It is also important to recognise when a horse is stressed, and to appreciate the effects this may have on his behaviour. Events or situations which we regard as normal some individuals may find very stressful indeed; such instances might include:

- Travelling
- Moving to a new home
- Having a new owner
- Meals not arriving on time
- The loss of a friend (horses do have their special friends)
- Weaning, which is a stressful time for both mare and foal
- Competing: some horses love it, others become very anxious about it; others who are talented may find they are being pushed too far, too fast (one event horse who was Advanced by the time he was six years old showed the degree of stress he felt by losing his tail hair)
- Being introduced to new field companions
- Being bullied as a result of being an inferior member of the herd

Many horses find travelling a stressful experience: a horse's natural instincts will make him suspicious and unhappy about going into the dark, confined space of a trailer. However, be patient, and he should soon learn to trust you

Relieving the Pain

If you suspect that your horse's problems are rooted in pain then you have to investigate further, perhaps with expert help either from a veterinary surgeon, an equine dentist or an equine 'back' man. In his work with 'difficult' horses to date, Max has found that a large proportion of pain-related problems can be traced to the horse's teeth, neck or quarters.

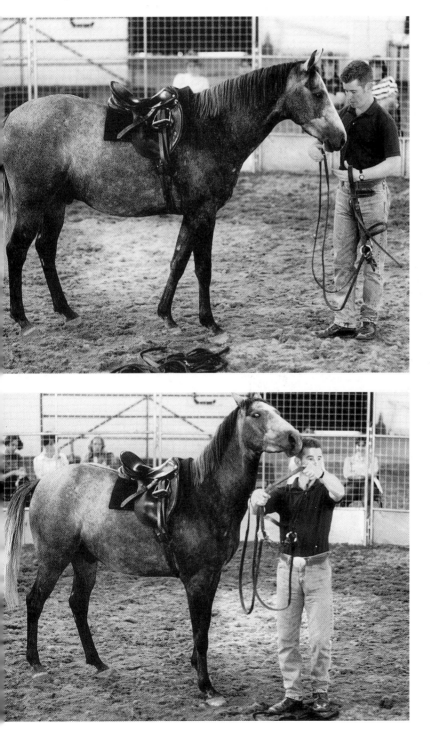

Max was working with this young gelding during a demonstration. He had been broken in the conventional way, but the rider was experiencing problems with him. Max joined up with him and he accepted the saddle quite happily. As a fairly big piece of equipment it is generally the saddle rather than the bridle which worries most horses. However, when the bridle was offered to this particular horse he immediately stuck his head in the air to avoid being bridled. Investigations by a master dentist revealed that he had teeth problems – even though he had been regularly attended by an equine dentist. It was not surprising therefore that he associated the bridle with the pain in his mouth and was reluctant to tolerate that particular piece of equipment

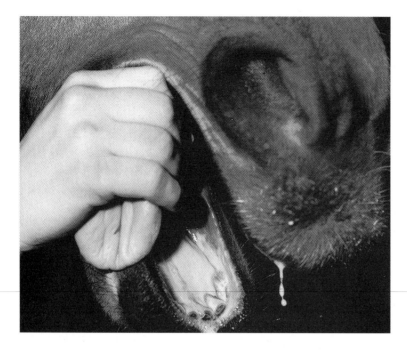

Practise getting hold of your horse's tongue and holding it out to the side of his mouth so that you can check on the condition of his teeth

Check the Teeth

Horse owners are advised in many books to check their horse's teeth regularly and to ensure that the teeth are rasped at least once a year (more often for older horses and horses under five). Dental care for horses may be carried out by vets or by equine 'dentists'. Vets will have had some formal training on equine teeth during their time at veterinary college, but there is at present no formal qualification for an equine dentist in Britain. There are currently only two master dentists and they gained their qualifications outside this country (the USA does have a training and qualification set-up for equine dentistry); this means that the 'dentists' that many owners are using for their horses are not formally qualified and the standard of work varies enormously. Some non-qualified dentists do provide a good service but others fail miserably and, of course, it is the horses which suffer. So how can owners decide what kind of service their horse is getting?

- When your vet or dentist next calls to check teeth, make sure that he does so using a gag, and that he uses it when rasping the teeth. Whilst this is not necessary for the whole procedure, it is vital if he is to get to the molars at the very back of the horse's mouth; if these are left unattended they can cause horrific injuries and soreness.
- Before your vet or dentist starts work he has to feel inside the horse's mouth to discover the extent of the dental problems. When he does this, ask if you can feel the teeth too, because then you can compare them later against the finished work.
- When the job is done, feel inside the horse's mouth very carefully: you should not be able to feel any sharp edges. If you can, then the dentist's performance has been poor.

Other signs of teeth problems are:

- Quidding, when the horse drops food from his mouth because it is sore, resulting in him being unable to chew his feed properly.
- Reluctance to be bridled.
- Reluctance to accept the bit when ridden; for example, the horse throws his head around and will not take a steady contact.
- Bad breath problems: these could indicate a tooth abcess.
- The horse takes longer to eat his feed – but otherwise does not display any other signs of ill-health.

Check the Neck and Back

Once any teeth problems are resolved, the horse's neck and back should be checked. Again, a large number of people offer their services as 'back' specialists – yet there are horrendous stories of so-called experts hitting horses' backs with huge mallets and suchlike to 'knock' a misplaced bone 'back in'. This is madness, because it is impossible to do this: between the withers and the loins there is no way that any of the vertebrae can be 'whacked back into place'. However, it is possible for some of the neck vertebrae to become

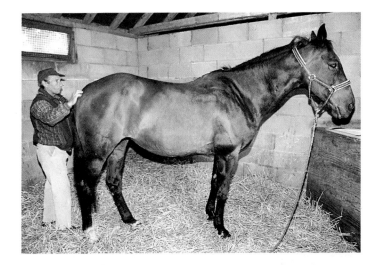

displaced, or for the horse's pelvis to be put out of alignment. Using the horse's own strength, these may be re-aligned: but this is not a job to be tackled by anyone. A thorough understanding and knowledge of equine anatomy is needed, as well as training and ability; so be quite certain of the credentials of those you let loose on your horse! There are reputable people about, and some centres specialise in offering such services: but ask your vet to recommend someone, or seek word-of-mouth references from people you respect for their horse knowledge; this is much better than relying on the recommendation of just anyone.

An important member of the team at the Maxwell yard is Andy Andrews who works on the horses' back and neck problems. Andy has extensive experience and helps the many horses who come into the yard with back and neck problems

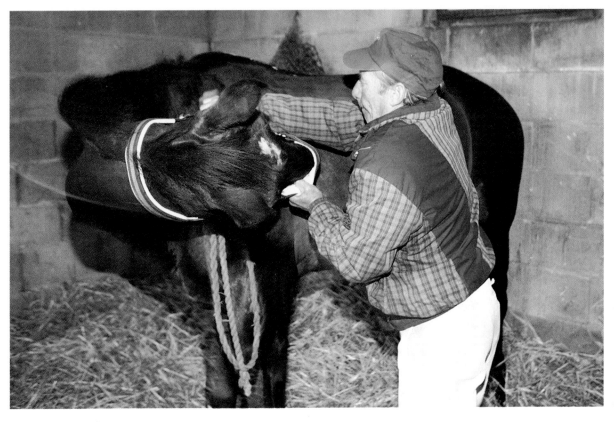

YOU AND YOUR FARRIER

If your horse has foot-related problems, your vet and farrier may need to work together. However, you can always assist your farrier by following some basic guidelines:

- provide a dry, preferably concreted, area for him to work in.
- ensure that your horse is waiting for him and has dry, clean legs and feet.
- ensure that your horse is used to having his feet picked up and will stand quietly.

Feet and the Farrier

Another person who has an important effect on your horse is the farrier – though, as always, the work of some is far better than that of others. However, no farrier can do a good job if you don't call upon his services. Unfortunately there are owners who are proud to tell you that their horse only needed the farrier four times last year; after all, the shoes didn't fall off, so why call the farrier more often?!   The horse's foot does, however, need regular attention from a qualified farrier every six weeks as a minimum, and often more regularly. The hoof grows from the coronet down, taking around nine months to grow from the coronary band to the toe. When the horse is exercised the hoof grows more quickly because the increased blood supply to the foot brings with it an increased supply of nutrients. Moreover, as exercise is increased, so is the horse's feed, and this also has an effect on hoof growth because more nutrients are being supplied. It is clear, therefore, why your farrier's attention is needed regularly, whether the horse is working or not.

Horses whose feet are neglected can have severe problems; most equine charities have photographs of animals whose hooves are so overgrown that they have curled up, and in some instances the only caring solution has been humane destruction. So regular visits from a farrier are vital – but it is important that your farrier does a good job, because poor shoeing can create its own problems and pain. A simple check is to look at the horse's coronary band: normally this would be straight across the front of the foot, tapering away to the heels but equally on each side. If the coronary band is uneven, however, this is sometimes a sign that the hoof is not properly balanced, as one side of the hoof is presumably coming into contact with the ground before the other. But before you launch into an argument with your farrier, do consider the horse's limb conformation, for this may also create uneven stresses on the foot. Watch the way the horse moves: if one side of the hoof is placed down before the other, then this uneven loading will be reflected by uneven coronary band growth.

A common problem is that of 'long toe, low heel' shoeing: this style causes considerable strain to be thrown onto the lower limb bones, tendons and ligaments, and it may lead to long-standing pain, such as navicular syndrome.

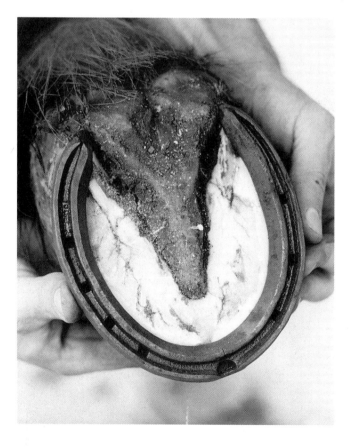

Regular footcare is essential for all horses, whether they are young or old, in work or resting

Conformation:
its Effect on Performance and Behaviour

The way in which a horse is put together has a dramatic effect on its athletic performance; it can also lead to painful situations. When assessing a horse's conformation it is important to allow yourself time to get an overall impression, before concentrating on individual details. Of course, each part of the horse interacts with and influences other parts, and individual conformational defects can predispose the horse to situations which could lead to discomfort or pain. But as well as recognising particular faults, it is vital to take into account a horse's overall make and shape in relation to the nature of the work he will be asked to do.

Should a horse be asked to perform tasks to which it is not particularly suited, then problems will arise. Take as an example the rider who evented her half-bred horse at Novice level with reasonable success. When it up-graded to Intermediate she was determined to continue, even though she knew that it had always struggled to make the time on the cross-country. However, she decided that getting it fitter was all that was needed. Unfortunately this was not the case: no matter how fit the horse was, it simply wasn't built to gallop as easily and efficiently as a full Thoroughbred. Thus when she tried to hurry it, she only succeeded in pushing it out of its stride, causing it to make

If your horse becomes unwilling and nappy, take a good look at him: his make and shape may not be suitable for the work you are asking him to do

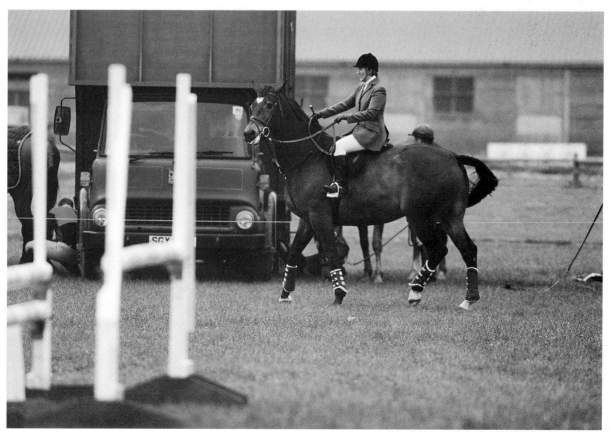

mistakes and so to lose confidence in its jumping. As a result it started to refuse, then became nappy; but the rider persisted with the fast work until eventually the horse broke down. Now it cannot be ridden for anything other than light work. Had the rider taken a step back in the first place, however, and looked at its conformation, and had she considered this in relation to her experiences when competing the horse, then she could have saved both herself and her horse a lot of pain.

So, consider your horse's conformation when asking him to undertake certain jobs. If he is built to be a showjumper, there is no point in trying to make him into a flat racer; and should you try, then at some point the defects in his make-up will throw up a major problem.

CONSIDER SOME OF THESE POINTS:

- A short, thick neck is seen in horses with draught or native blood in them: think of an Irish Draught and compare it to a Thoroughbred. The strong neck of the former was needed because the animal was used extensively on farms, performing many jobs as a draught horse; it was only later that it became used as a riding animal. Thoroughbreds, however, have always been bred for their speed, hence the long, narrow neck.

- A horse's stride length is affected by the length of the neck: a short neck limits foreleg movement; too long a neck could also mean extra weight on the horse's forehand and therefore increased stress on the forelegs. Such horses tend to be rather heavy in the rider's hands.

- Stride length has repercussions on the wear and tear on the horse's limbs, since a short, choppy stride means extra concussion on the legs and feet.

- The way in which the neck is set on is also influential: thus a low-set neck restricts the movement of the shoulder and so the stride length, placing the horse on the forehand.

- A ewe neck (which resembles a long-drawn-out S) results in the horse having a high head carriage, and the knock-on effect of this is a hollowing of the back which makes it difficult for it to bring its hindquarters underneath its body. The quarters therefore trail out behind, making it impossible for the rider to engage them effectively, and the result is an unbalanced,

uncomfortable ride – and the horse does not find this particularly comfortable either! It may have been in discomfort since its early years, and had this been recognised, then it might have been possible to have remedied the situation – and if this is the case for a lot of such horses, then probably they need not have become ewe-necked at all.

- Low withers make it difficult to fit a saddle, and both saddle and rider will slip forwards readily; this can bruise the withers if they are not particularly well muscled.

- A sloping shoulder is considered to be beneficial, the ideal being that it slopes at an angle of 45° to the ground. If the angle between the scapula (shoulder bone) and the humerus (arm bone) is greater than 90°, and preferably exceeding this by at least 10°, then the horse will have more swing of the forearm and its stride will be longer and freer, enabling it to cover the ground with less effort and fatigue than a horse with a more upright shoulder.

- Short pasterns cannot absorb shock so easily, so the horse is more susceptible to concussion; this can predispose to certain problems such as navicular. The onset of this disease takes place over some time, during which the horse will start to exhibit certain tell-tale signs, for example a shortening of the stride and discomfort when jumping, possibly showing as a refusal to jump.

- A long back makes it more difficult for the horse to engage his hindquarters, whilst a short back limits his scope.

SUMMARY

- If you compete regularly, your horse should be checked by a reputable 'back person' every six weeks because after this length of time it is common to find one or more trapped nerves. Showjumpers generally suffer in front because they have to snap up their forelegs and round their back to such a degree; with horses on the forehand, on the other hand, such as National Hunt horses, it is generally the back end which is out of alignment. Pleasure horses should be checked on an annual basis.

- Sports horses make tremendous use of their heads and necks, probably 70 per cent as compared to the rest of their body.

- Showjumpers will still be able to jump even if their back end is out of true, but if the front end is out they cannot jump.

- Rearing may indicate problems in front of the saddle.

- Bucking may indicate problems behind the saddle.

- The horse's hips, too, can be misaligned: look at the hip bones on each side, and you may be able to see a difference.

- Think carefully about the horse's conformation: so often we say, 'Oh, he's always like that': but it could be that the horse cannot move properly because of a problem; for example, one horse we had looked as if she was wearing a wet nappy because she was moving in such a restricted way, but this was all due to a *neck* problem.

- Consider whether the horse is muscled up, and has the appearance implied by its breeding. For example, we knew a horse which was half Irish Draught but looked extremely weedy. It transpired that it was suffering neck and muscular pain, however, and was unable to move properly, and so its hindquarters, topline and neck had little muscular development. If a horse does not look or move as you would expect considering its breeding, then ask yourself why.

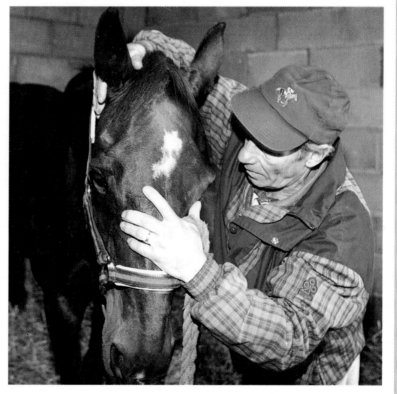

Be sure of your 'back person's' credentials because there are many 'quacks' about. However, a reputable back specialist will have a thorough understanding and knowledge of the equine anatomy, his manipulative skills will be in demand countrywide both for the racehorse worth a fortune and for the ordinary family cob

SUMMARY

- Smell the horse's breath: this is a useful indicator of tooth troubles. When a horse is experiencing problems with its teeth – as may be the case in particular with youngsters which are changing their teeth or older horses with long hooks on their teeth – it is generally because these are damaging the soft flesh which becomes putrid, so producing bad breath.
- A horse salivating in its box – it looks as if it is blowing bubbles – is telling you it has teeth problems.
- Other signs of teeth problems include the following:
  The horse looks as if it is mouthing in its box.
  It jerks its bit around; generally this indicates the presence of hooks on the teeth.
  It plunges when you take up the rein contact.
- Teeth should be checked every six to eight months in horses up to five years old, as there are so many changes which occur in the teeth in this time. Six-monthly checks are advisable for older horses, and yearly checks for others.
- Have wolf teeth taken out as soon as possible.
- It may cost more for a good dentist but it is a sound investment, and will save the horse years of pain.
- Other signs of pain are a wrinkly face, and when the tongue lolls out.
- The top horse people are learning constantly, and so can all of us: it is a closed mind which is the real enemy of horses.
- A horse in pain or discomfort will adopt a completely different outline. For example, Max has seen a three-year-old which was so uptight you would have thought it had been ridden for many years; in fact it was unbroken.
- If we injure or tweak ourselves, then as a rule we hold ourselves incorrectly; a horse does just the same, but unlike us it cannot say in words that it is hurt and it is up to us to recognise the non-verbal signs.

This horse is not using itself very efficiently, and this, together with the resistance in the mouth, merits further investigation

- People become accustomed to how a horse looks, and sometimes they don't even think about whether it is an odd shape. Accustom yourself to looking at your horse with fresh eyes each day so that you can realise when something is wrong.
- Learn to assess different breeds: for example Thoroughbreds usually look quite lean, whereas Warmbloods are big and round. Get to know what any particular breed is meant to look like, then you will know whether your horse is falling short of what is expected, and you can start to find out why.
- Pain that shows in the back is displaced pain – often because a vertebra is out in the neck.

SUMMARY

■ Sometimes a horse may not behave badly all the time, and in this circumstance some people refuse to acknowledge that its intermittently bad behaviour may be rooted in pain. It is important to pay attention to your horse in every way: watch him when he moves, as he comes in and out of the stable, as he goes off into the field; watch him coming towards and going away from you, video him, get a friend to trot him up for you so you can see how he moves. Start to look with different eyes. Stand him up and look at how he positions his legs and feet; as he walks towards you and halts he will take up a certain stance, but if he is then asked to back up he may stand differently: is this an awkward position for him? Something that needs investigating further?

This mare suffered pain for a considerable time. Compare her way of going here with the next picture

■ To check for pain, for example where the brachiocephalic muscle (which runs along the neck from the head) goes into the shoulder area, press your thumb in; the horse will undoubtedly react if something is not as it should be. Check underneath the belly in the girth area by running your fingers across the muscle; he may swing his head round because of discomfort there.

■ A simple incidence may have resulted in pain: for instance the horse may have slipped, missed his footing, gone on his forehand, fallen off the lorry ramp or down the steps into his stable. This sort of thing will send shock waves up his body, in the same way that it does to us when, for instance, we think there is another step to go and there isn't.

Horses don't reason as to why they are in pain in the way that we do: they just adjust themselves to cope with the pain and discomfort – for example, one leg will take a shorter step – and will move in the best way they can to accommodate their suffering.

A much happier horse: Andy worked on her neck problems and Max then helped the mare to realise that she no longer needed to run away from pain

■ If a horse believes that when you get on his back he will be made uncomfortable, then he will find a way of coping with that discomfort; and if it involves changing his gait, then he will do so.

■ Trying to impose normal daily activities on a horse that is suffering pain, let alone extracurricular activities such as going to small shows, will create tremendous stress. The more genuine types of horse will labour on; a horse that is not so tolerant will explode.

ESTABLISHING TRUST: 'JOIN-UP'

The first thing to resolve when dealing with a 'difficult' or badly behaved horse is why it is reacting in the particular way it is. With so many horses coming through his yard, Max now appreciates that certain patterns of behaviour are caused by pain in particular areas. For instance, a horse will often rear as a result of pain in the neck or mouth, and he will buck if he suffers back pain. Horses which pull are also generally running away from pain, and the teeth of a puller are checked first.

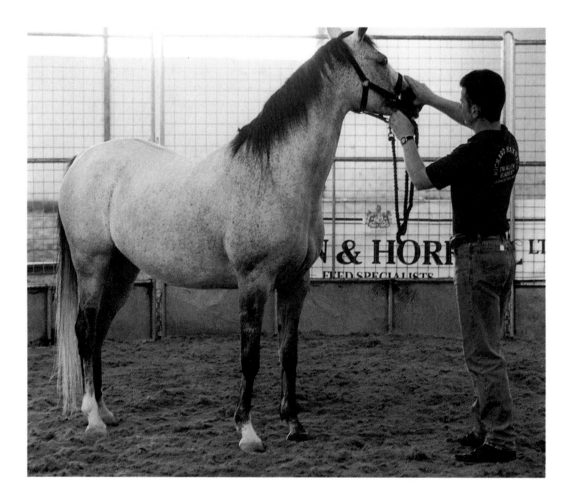

There is little point in starting to work with any horse until

the source of the pain has been removed; and even when his neck, back or teeth are obviously clinically 'better', he will still have a clear memory of the pain so it is unreasonable to expect that in some miraculous way he will start behaving immediately. Basically he has to be re-educated, and the first step along this route is the establishment of mutual respect and trust: we call this 'joining up' with the horse.

Although perhaps best known at present for helping problem horses, Max's knowledge of equine behaviour means that he can create situations where the horse has the best possible chance to learn to oblige his handler, and most importantly, to do so by his own choice. By keying in to the horse's communications system, Max can read the signals being sent by any horse and can use his own body language to assert his position at the top of the equine hierarchy.

Demonstrating passive body language: low, rounded shoulders, bowed head, no eye-to-eye contact with the horse, arms at the side

An aggressive stance: overall a bigger appearance because the arms are lifted out to the sides, the head is up, eye contact with the horse is maintained and the shoulders are held high and square

The 'Joining-up' of Man and Horse

Max works his horses in a round pen which is 50 to 60ft (15 to 18m) in diameter and about 8ft (2.5m) high. He has no need for whips or any other artificial aid: it is just him and the horse. When giving demonstrations Max is always anxious to point out that what happens in the pen is quite predictable and is obvious to see: he has found that many people have come to a much better understanding of equine communication just by observing. The outer ring of the pen is the 'bad' place to be because here the horse has to work, trotting or cantering

Checking for mouth problems: this is one of the first things which should be done with a 'difficult' horse

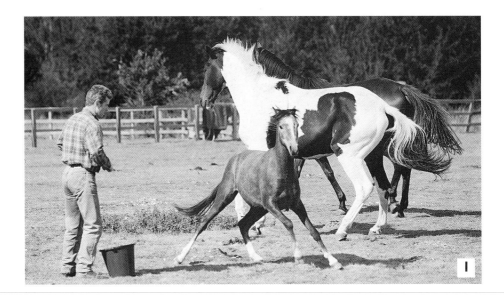

1 *Putting the aggressive stance into action: in spite of the lure of the food bucket, the horses respect the fact that Max's body language is saying that he is at the top of the pecking order*

2 *The coloured horse is normally the leader in this field, but he gives way to Max*

3 *Adopting passive body language. Max is not seen as a threat by the horses and is allowed to wander amongst them without much notice being paid to him*

around; using his body language Max can 'banish' the horse to the outside. He does this by making himself appear aggressive by adopting a big, square stance, by keeping his head up and maintaining eye contact with the horse. Max stays in the centre of the pen, the 'good' place to be. His method relies on the fact that horses are gregarious creatures and will always seek company, even if it is human rather than equine. He has no treats with which to bribe the horse into the centre: if it submits and chooses to come to Max, its only reward will be his company.

Using his body language and with the help of a soft line which he throws towards the horse, Max keeps it moving on the outer circle. The horse is following its own instinct, that is, it is using flight to distance itself from the predator (Max). During this time Max watches its body language carefully: some horses will have a very tight, tense mouth indicating anxiety, others are less anxious but

Max works horses in a round pen which is ideal for this method of starting a horse. This type of pen can also be erected outside, but it is important that the ground conditions are good

more puzzled about this strange-looking creature, perhaps wondering whether it wishes to communicate.

Gradually Max will close down the horse's options for flight: for instance, he will block its path, simply by standing there and with his body language indicating that he is the predator. This causes the horse to turn and flee in the opposite direction. Max will then block its flight on this rein, and will keep doing this until the horse starts to think about its other available options: in other words it can continue to flee, or it can decide to submit to this 'predator'.

Invariably as it makes its way round, on its own, on the outside circle, a horse will at some point start to show that it does want Max's company. Initially these signs of submission may be very subtle: a flick of the inside ear in his direction, or a glance towards him; then certain movements of the mouth or licking the lips, and eventually a lowering of the head and neck. Gradually it makes the circles smaller, and

WORKING IN A SUITABLE AREA

Max works in a pen, but many people will not have this facility. Access to an indoor school can usually be arranged; many centres hire out their schools for a relatively small charge per horse per hour. You will need to block off or 'round off' the corners of the school, for example by using jump wings and poles: this ensures that the horse doesn't get himself stuck in a corner, refusing to come out. It is possible to achieve join-up by working in an indoor school in this way but as the working area is larger you need to be much fitter!

The horse has decided, on its own initiative, to entrust itself to Max's company, and is completely submissive: it now craves physical contact and is rewarded with pats and scratches, and will follow Max closely wherever he goes

41

finally it will stop and turn inwards, ready to give up and come in off the outer circle.

Max continues to wait, however, until the horse makes the next big step and decides, on its own initiative, to approach him. At this point Max is very careful that his body language reassures the horse, adopting a non-aggressive posture by dropping his head and rounding his shoulders. The horse now craves physical contact with Max; and when it has come close enough it is rewarded with pats and scratches.

The horse has to conclude for itself that being with Max is the better option. Sometimes horses come towards him and then decide to leave again; Max does not punish them for this, but he does make them accountable for their decisions and actions, sending them forwards around the pen using his 'aggressive' body language. When, on the other hand, a horse decides to come forwards offering communication, obviously letting Max know that it wants to make contact with him, then Max adopts a passive stance.

Basically, in order to appreciate the 'comfortable' status quo – that is, being with Max – the horse has to know what is uncomfortable: so if he chooses flight, then he is made to experience fear and isolation, and it is up to him to decide if and when he wants to come back into the 'comfort zone', in other

1 Working in the round pen, the outside is the 'bad' place to be where the horse is alone and has to work. If he chooses to leave Max at any time this is where he will be sent to – by choosing flight he has to work, alone, on the outer circle. Max sends him out by adopting an aggressive stance

2 Gradually the horse's flight loses impetus and he will eventually signal to Max that he would like to negotiate a new deal; the signs are always the same and can be seen by people watching. Initially it may be a flick of his inside ear towards Max, the next stage will be motions of licking and chewing which effectively say 'I'm not aggressive because I'm licking and chewing and can't do that and bite you!'. Eventually he will lower his head and neck, signalling submission and that he wants to come in towards Max

3

3 *Once the horse makes this decision Max adopts a passive posture. This can be the tricky part for some horses because they are not yet quite sure that they want to take the next step and approach Max. Some turn away, and because they have chosen to flee, Max adopts an aggressive posture, sending them out onto the larger circle again, making them accountable for their decision to turn away*

words by returning to Max. This all sounds simple enough and may give the impression that it is a quick procedure; but it may in fact take anything from a few minutes to several sessions over many days.

Each horse is different, and its reaction in the pen is very much governed by its life experiences. Youngsters with largely good experience of human contact will join up with handlers very quickly, whereas older horses whose dealings with humans have been traumatic will be much more sceptical; they may approach, but will fly off again as soon as they are touched. However, it has been their decision to banish themselves to the outer circle, and it will also be their decision as to when they approach Max again.

Sometimes it takes days for a difficult horse to submit and treat Max with complete confidence. However, once it has made its decision it will keep its half of the agreement! Just as humans are generally

4 *When the horse makes the conscious decision to approach Max and comes close enough he is rewarded with the physical contact he desires, being patted and scratched. Again, some horses find this a bit too much and fly off, and have to work on the lonely outer circle again until they decide to submit*

more enthusiastic about doing something which is their own idea, so horses are happy to follow a path *they* have chosen, rather than doing something because they have been forced along that route.

Having made friends with Max, a horse will follow him everywhere; because he has made it plain that he is at the top of the equine hierarchy, it will follow his lead. Thus bad loaders will happily accompany him into lorries and trailers, and

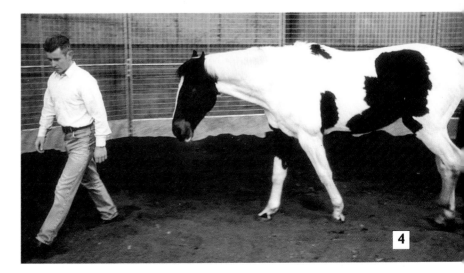

4

Once a horse has confidence in you there is tremendous scope for both horse and rider/handler to enjoy new experiences

racehorses will no longer refuse to go into the starting stalls. Horses will also learn in the pen that as herd leader, Max must be treated with due respect, and this is useful when dealing with those which have become accustomed to taking charge of their owners and bossing them around. In the pen they realise that Max also has his 'personal space', and just as a horse would not dream of entering another's space without invitation, so they will not invade Max's space unless invited. This is a valuable lesson for over-confident and curious youngsters; and once learned, they do not jeopardise the privilege of being in Max's company by behaving badly.

From this position, Max can then put his authority to the test by insisting that the horse lets him into its vulnerable areas: along the crest of its neck, under the belly, between the eyes. Allowing a human to do this represents a great step forwards for, in the wild, horses would be attacked by predators jumping on their backs and clamping their teeth around their neck. Knowing how much a domesticated horse is still ruled by its instincts, you can appreciate that to let a human take hold of its neck is a big step indeed, because it is thereby putting trust for you above its instincts.

This applies to so much that we do with horses; for example, picking up one of its feet means that the horse is left in a very vulnerable position; rugging up, tacking up and allowing a rider on its back are amazing demonstrations of trust when you consider the horse's instinctive reaction to strange things or to an intruder on its back.

'Joining up' with a horse can be used by anyone to improve his or her relationship with their own. Having worked on a problem horse and resolved its difficulties, Max then helps the owner to become aware of the animal's psychology and how to key into it so that the partnership can continue with a firm foundation.

Countless other problems can be worked on once Max has the horse's confidence; his experience has shown that real rogue horses rarely exist, whereas many do suffer pain; by misbehaving they are trying to tell their owners that they hurt and they do this in a variety of ways such as bucking, refusing to jump, pulling faces – there are countless ways in which a horse tries to get his message across. The crucial step for the owner is to realise that he *can* understand his horse, if only he were to listen.

SUMMARY

- The horse's language is one which humans can learn – and every horse will then understand you.

- Each horse is an individual: some will 'talk' loudly, others will only whisper, and you will probably need advice from a more experienced 'communicator' in order to appreciate what some horses are saying.

- Courses are available with Richard Maxwell whereby you can learn much more, on a practical basis, about communication with your horse.

- Joining up should be undertaken in a safe, confined area. Although experienced people such as Max can keep a horse's concentration in a large area in spite of other distractions, this is not easy, nor is it recommended.

- Remember that communication is a two-way process: thus you have to allow your horse to 'speak', and to listen to what he is saying.

- In Max's experience the sex of the horse makes little difference as regards its attitude towards joining up. Dominant mares can be hard work; in the wild it is the dominant mare of the herd, and not the stallion, which makes all the decisions. Max has found that stallions are extremely rewarding to work with as they are so intelligent and so willing to co-operate with him.

- Remember there are no rights or wrongs for the horse with this system; thus he is not actively punished with the whip or spurs. His only 'punishment' if he makes the wrong decision is to be denied the 'comfort zone' – the company of his human.

Trust established, 'join-up' achieved: by allowing a human to take hold of his head, the horse is putting himself in a very vulnerable position – this is a truly remarkable demonstration of trust

'STARTING':
FROM FOAL TO FULL GROWN

There are many different views on 'starting' or breaking in a horse; opinions vary within the same region of one country, never mind across the horse-owning peoples of the world! The methods described here are therefore just one way of approaching this process; also we use the expression 'start' in preference to 'break in' as the latter carries with it connotations of force, resistance and submission. What this book aims to show is that by working with, and understanding the horse, a true partnership can be achieved with the minimum of adverse activity on either side.

Birth and First Steps

When a foal is born in the wild it is on its feet within an hour and is standing, walking and feeding from the right place (with a little help from Mum). A short while later it can canter, follow its mother and call out if it loses her. By the next day it will be moving easily at all paces, getting up and down in a more co-ordinated way and be nibbling at grass.

It is vital that the foal learns so quickly because in a wild state the horse, being a prey animal, has to be mobile in order to survive. A mare with a new-born foal is usually extremely protective, and this is nature's way of ensuring that the bond between mare and foal is established. During the first hour of the foal's life a process known as imprinting will occur: this is a rapid irreversible learning process when basically the mare learns that the foal is hers and the foal learns to identify its mother. When a mare has foaled it is important not to disturb this imprinting process.

However, work with foal imprinting is being done whereby in the first sixty to ninety minutes of life the handler will stroke the foal's vulnerable areas – the belly, between the eyes, the ears and the legs – he will insert his fingers into its mouth, perhaps insert a thermometer; aluminium foil will be scrunched up over its body and its feet will be handled. The people involved in this project do each task fifty times and the aim is to ensure that the foal will happily accept human contact.

The Early Days

It is common practice for foals bred in a domesticated situation to have a foal slip (headcollar) put on within the first few days. The foals are turned out to grass each day and will follow alongside their dams; the next step is to lead them with the help of perhaps an old towel round their neck, and only then progress to leading them in their foal slips. However, whilst this ensures that the foal is handled, it has not truly 'broken' it to the halter, or taught it respect for the headcollar or halter. It will resent the restraint of the halter instinctively and will not respond to pressure from it: it may tolerate it, but that is all. The first lesson therefore has to be submission to the halter.

In addition to the foal slip you will require a long lead rope, and a handkerchief knotted onto the end of a stick. The lead rope is passed around the foal's neck, fastened with a non-slip knot so that it cannot become too tight, and then the end is fed through the ring at the back of the foal slip; like this, the handler has more control and the action of the halter is more definite.

The handkerchief on the stick is used to tickle the foal's quarters whilst pressure is applied on the halter, the objective being that the foal learns to move away from the irritation and submits to the pressure on the halter. Initially the foal will probably pull back but the pressure must be retained, and as soon as it ceases to resist and takes a step, however small, in the right direction, it is rewarded by the handler. This reward is given in the form of instant relief from the halter pressure, a rub between the eyes and a kind word.

The procedure is repeated until the foal moves happily away from the handkerchief into the headcollar on both the left and the right reins. Thus without the handler resorting to bully tactics or anything frightening, the foal has learnt that the best way out of an unpleasant situation – the handkerchief tickling his quarters and pressure on the halter – is to move towards the handler and therefore a removal of the pressure.

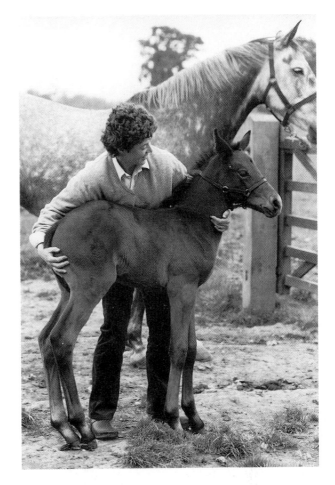

You can never start too young: this youngster has accepted a foal slip on its head, and therefore could now be shown how to truly respect it and to always walk into pressure. This is an invaluable lesson for the future as it makes tying up easy

◀ *Although a foal would soon be tired by too much mental stimulus, you can teach it some easy lessons which will stand it in good stead for the rest of its life*

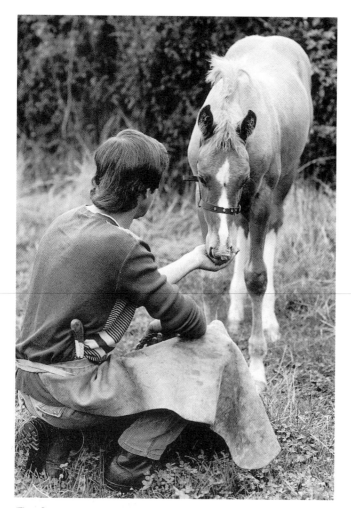

The farrier has an important role to play in a horse's life and first impressions set the tone for the following years. You can prepare your young foal by handling its legs regularly and teaching it to pick up its feet

Once the foal has made this choice he is happy to take the easy way out and follow the handler wherever he or she happens to go. It is vital when doing this that the handler suppresses his instinctive impulse to take hold of the rope close to the foal's head: let the foal have freedom of his head. And however small the step towards the handler, there must be immediate relief from pressure and a reward for the foal.

Watch the foal's eyes and ears for signs that he will submit to you. A glance in your direction, an ear pointing towards you, if he licks his lips, all these are indications that the foal's inclination is towards you. Whilst all this is happening the mare needs to be held nearby – but even with the dam close by, the foal soon realises that stepping towards his handler is preferable to resisting and causing himself discomfort.

This important lesson of submitting to pressure and coming into the halter pays dividends later, for example when the foal is tied up. Putting a halter on the foal and leading him round from both the nearside and the offside can then become a regular part of his life.

Keep these sessions short and sweet, however, only about five minutes at the most, because his young mind cannot cope with too much. At this age the foal will readily absorb new experiences and store them in his mind for future reference; this will apply to bad experiences as well as to good ones, so the onus is on the trainer to create situations and conditions in which the horse can learn positive things.

Without wishing to be controversial, it is my experience that whenever a horse has to be subjected to something less pleasant such as examination when he is in pain, or vaccinations, these tasks are usually carried out by a man. As a result many horses do associate men with their less pleasant experiences and may therefore resent them, and this needs to be considered when you accustom your young horse to human contact. It is a good idea to introduce different people to the horse, particularly the professionals with whom he will almost certainly come into contact in the future, but if these are males then both you and they may need to allow plenty of time and have a very patient attitude in order to compensate for the horse's suspicious view of men.

What Next?

Basically you now have a choice: continue to handle your foal regularly and prepare him well for various events in his life; or turn him away and do the minimum with him.

Any foal will have to be wormed and have his feet trimmed regularly, as well as have his inoculations, and it seems rather unfair to keep dragging him out of the field and subjecting him to something relatively unpleasant without any preparatory handling whatsoever. Think about it: whether you are throwing a dinner party or taking an exam, everything goes much more smoothly and successfully if you prepare in advance, and the same goes for your foal's experiences.

Horses have certain vulnerable areas on their bodies and are instinctively reluctant to let other horses and humans into these: you have to be a trusted friend to be allowed access to these parts. When they are young, however, they are much more open about giving you access, so it makes sense to show a youngster that being touched under the belly, having his ears caressed and being rubbed between the eyes and down the legs is a pleasurable sensation and an acceptable part of his relationship with you.

Expose a foal to as many good experiences as possible whilst it is young and impressionable; for instance, you can prevent it being neurotic about rustling bags or sudden noises by letting it investigate such things in its own time. While you want to enjoy a good relationship with your horses, it is important that the balance is 51 per cent in your favour

Stroking the foal's legs regularly, for example, will make things much easier when it needs the attention of a farrier. It is difficult enough for a youngster to realise that it *can* balance on three legs, without the added trauma of having its legs touched for the first time. Investing a little time at the start of your horse's life will save much grief later – and make a friend of your farrier who will play an important part throughout your horse's life.

Foals also enjoy being scratched all over, and working over their bodies in this way prepares them for other people handling them, for instance the vet when he needs to inject them.

There is also no reason why the foal should not learn about other aspects of life, for instance loading into a lorry or trailer, visiting a show just to see the sights and sounds, trotting over a pole on the ground alongside Mum – provided, of course, that she will happily go over poles: remember that foals learn very readily from their mother's behaviour, so you do not want a demonstration from Mum of 'I can't possibly go near that monster!'

Obviously everything has to be done in moderation, as the foal's young mind and body can easily become tired: but a little positive stimulus for your foal will help to lay a good foundation for his future.

Weaning

The most traumatic time for a foal comes when he is weaned from his mother, usually around the age of six months. When they are separated there will be distress and anxiety on the part of both mare and foal – but this would also happen in the wild, where there would generally be another foal on the way causing the mare's milk to dry up and the mare herself to distance herself from the older foal.

Once the foal is separated from its mother it will seek comfort, and this is where you, as owner or handler, can play an important part. By 'joining up' with the foal again you can re-establish all your earlier work and focus the foal's attention on you rather than its dam. Spend a great deal of time with your foal immediately after it has been weaned as it will need your comfort and support.

You could introduce bits to young horses – even as yearlings – but do keep an eye on them to ensure that nothing happens to frighten them. At this age, they are very impressionable and you want their view on life to be positive and pleasant, or you'll create problems for the future

Occasionally foals which are left to wean naturally are still looking to their dams for support when they ought to be 'grown up'; for instance we knew one six-year-old horse which still went everywhere with mother!

Yearlings

Regular handling can carry on throughout the horse's early life: whilst you do not want to impose hard physical work upon him, there is no reason why a yearling could not be introduced to new experiences such

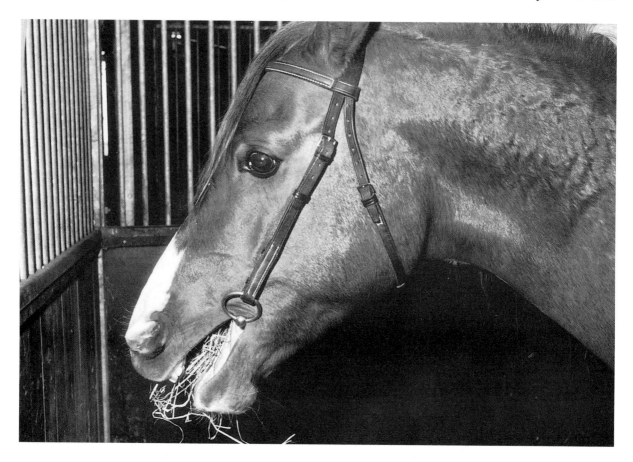

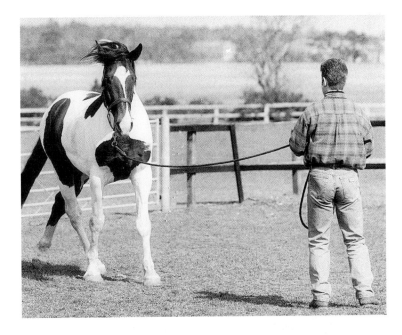

as wearing boots, a roller and a pad on his back, even a rug. Take care that all experiences are positive ones, and be sure that the situations and the environment which you create are set up in such a way that he accepts learning happily.

When introducing new experiences to your youngster you need to be positive. Sometimes trying to be quiet and sympathetic may make a horse more nervous; often it is anxiety about what you are about to do, rather than what you actually do, that sets him on edge. How often have you found yourself worrying more in anticipation of an event, than the event itself warranted when it actually happened?

Thus on the one hand you try and give your young horse a stimulating experience of some sort, say, two or three times a week. The alternative is that he is left just loafing about in a field all the time – and leaving him in a field for the first three or four years of his life is not doing him any favours. It is rather like allowing a young child to run riot and to misbehave at home, and then sending it off to boarding school where it is expected to live by certain rules. What generally happens is that the child rebels. Similarly, if a young horse has enjoyed a wild and carefree existence in a field, and then at four years old is suddenly expected to work for twenty minutes on the lunge with just a week or two of preparation for this complete change in lifestyle, it may well object, and violently! And if a young horse learns to use its power and strength against you, then you will have a major problem in asserting your authority. If you own a horse you should be committed to doing right by it, and it is undoubtedly far better to invite it to enjoy a wide range of experiences throughout its early life; then when the serious business of work begins, it is ready and willing to take up the challenge.

Respect for the halter should be instilled into the horse very early on: at the slightest pressure on the halter rope he should be happy to walk on, or to walk up to his handler calmly and sensibly; he should not pull back, or run on ahead, or barge about, but should know that once the halter is put on, he must behave with decorum

Mouthing the Young Horse

Although each horse has to be treated as an individual, mouthing a youngster – introducing it to the bit – can be carried out when the horse is two-and-a-half years old. In recent years stainless steel has become the accepted material for bits as this sort is easier to clean and lasts longer. However, we have found that horses benefit from the use of black iron and copper for mouthing bits. Bits with keys encourage the horse to play with the bit, get his tongue over it, under it, loll his tongue out of the side of his mouth – in other words, anything but

For safety reasons, work in an enclosed area when your horse is first worked on long lines. The handler should wear gloves and it is also advisable to wear a hat

actually to take hold of it. By contrast a black iron and copper bit does encourage him to bite it and mouth on it – and after all, when we ride him we want him to take the bit in a steady contact, so why not prepare him for this at an early age? To start with, it is as well to fasten a leather coupling strap between the bit rings and under the horse's jaw; this prevents him turning the bit over, and stops it pulling through his mouth.

Work on Two Lines (Long-lining)

Between the ages of two and three a horse could also be introduced to short sessions on the lunge, in walk and trot; these might build up to a maximum of ten minutes. Too much lungeing is to be avoided since it places considerable strain on the joints and limbs.

Many people lunge using just one rein, but this can have a particularly unbalancing effect on the horse. Also, unless you are lungeing in a round pen it is inevitable that he will lean towards the arena entrance or field gate, so you have to feed line out, gather it up again and so on, the result being that he will not have been lunged particularly well.

It is also inevitable that at some point during the lungeing session the horse will become unbalanced, and the handler's instinctive reaction is to lift up the lunge line rather sharply – which makes the horse even more unbalanced. In addition, the heavy cavesson and the weight of the lunge line encourage the horse to lean on it, so his head is turned to the outside of the circle.

Increased control and more effective lungeing can be achieved by using two reins, the outside rein brought behind the horse's quarters; continue to work on a circle. By using his body language as well as the two lines Max can control the horse easily, teaching it to stop and to turn when it feels the lightest of pressure on the reins; there is certainly no need to haul on them to produce turns and stops. Working on transitions in this way helps a youngster to learn how to balance itself, and how to use its hindquarters properly; so by the time a rider gets on board it will have learnt some valuable lessons already and will be able to adjust more easily to carrying the extra weight.

Using two lines in this way is also more productive than spending hours long-reining the horse around the countryside. Whilst long-reining may reassure the future rider, simply because the horse has been introduced to stimuli such as traffic, the horse which has established a relationship with his handler and has worked in a round pen will be just as prepared for the next step: being ridden.

There is a school of thought that being long-lined in the countryside helps the horse's education, but the basic tools of control can be just as easily learned in an enclosed area, and the horse's training then continued there until he is ready to be ridden out

More Serious Work

Young horses soon become bored, and can then become cheeky and rather big for their boots. It is therefore more profitable to keep stimulating their minds. When dealing with youngsters there is often the tendency to take things slowly, but this can work against you when you have a bright horse all ready to soak up new experiences. If you fail to keep the interest of horses like this they may well start using their brains against you.

Introducing new experiences to the horse throughout his young life means that when the time comes actually to back him, the process is just an extension of the whole relationship and partnership that you have built up. Think of backing him along the lines of your partnership entering a new stage; this also gets away from the idea of the breaking process being one in which the horse is dominated by the handler. After all, you and the horse ought to be sharing the responsibility of the breaking or starting process, as it affects both of you and your future lives.

Most horses accept the process of having the bridle put on quite happily if they have been properly prepared; thus horses which Max starts are mouthed well in advance of being backed

Hundreds of young horses have been started successfully by Richard Maxwell, whose approach is quite different to the more traditional route followed by most people: first he will lie across the

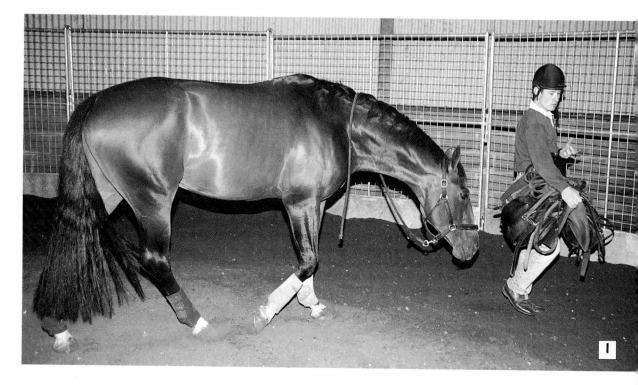

horse's back, introducing the idea of being ridden to the horse, *before* he puts on the saddle; and he will do this entirely unaided. The important thing is that by the time Max is ready to back a horse he will already have established a good relationship with it, communicating with it using a language it understands. The horse is obviously comfortable with Max, allowing him to enter its personal space and happy to let him have access to its vulnerable areas, its neck and back, and under its belly and legs.

As the horses accept him so readily it is simply another small step for them to allow Max on to their back: they have decided to trust him, and he has never let them down. Working as usual in his round pen, Max takes note of where, on the circle, a horse makes most of its signals (ear flicking, lip chewing, dropping his head); it will tend to send these to Max from the same area, and it is in this area that Max will choose to start the backing process.

As we have indicated, Max departs from the traditional ways of backing in that no one restrains the horse and no one helps to leg him up so he can lie across the horse's back. With his method, however, the horse tends to exhibit some curiosity but very little anxiety, largely because it feels entirely unpressured, and because it knows that if it wants to leave Max's company it can do so. Most horses, though, once they have decided to join up with Max, prefer to stay in his presence. Once Max is lying over the horse's back he allows it to explore him. Those who have handled youngsters will appreciate that once they have had the chance to touch and sniff a strange object they will often then give it no more than a passing glance.

1 This young horse, a stallion, is having its first experience of tack and a rider. The process started with Max joining up with him and as you can see, he is very committed to being with Max and happily follows him

2 Max works without restraining the horse. As he is happy to let Max touch his vulnerable areas and trusts him, he is not concerned when the saddle is placed on him. He is sent out to the outer circle of the pen and worked so that he can experience its feel

3 The bridle poses no problems, the horse having been mouthed for a few days before backing

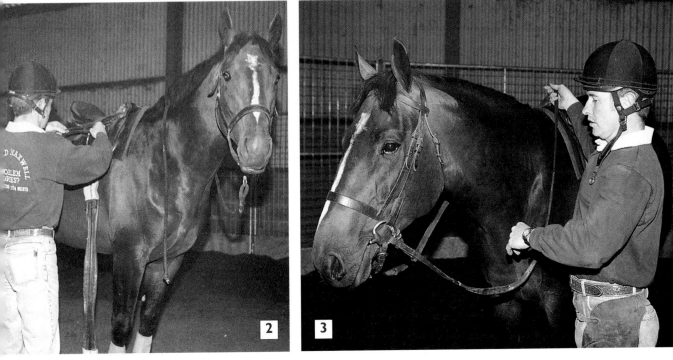

Max spends time 'backing' the horse from both sides until it accepts his presence completely. The reason for working on both sides is that when a rider is astride the horse, its wide vision means that it can see the person on both sides – therefore it is as well that the horse is used to this sensation at an early stage.

Once the horse is used to having some weight on its back, Max introduces the saddle, and since it has no reason to mistrust him, so it accepts its feel. Max will then send the horse out to work around the pen so that it can become thoroughly used to the feel of wearing tack. Its natural instincts will tell it to get rid of the object on its back so it is not uncommon for it to buck like mad as it goes round the pen. It was interesting to watch Max back three young horses on a demonstration evening: two of the three bucked and twisted for two circuits of the pen, then stopped and just accepted the saddle; the third, which had been remarkably laid back throughout the earlier processes, continued to be so when the saddle was placed on it – it simply said OK, and didn't react at all.

One of the horses which bucked had shown a degree of uncertainty when the saddle pad and then the saddle was first placed on his back. Max carries out this work with the horse unrestrained so it is free to leave at any time; in fact this particular horse did decide to run off, so he deftly removed the saddle and used his body language to send it around the outside of the pen, so making the *horse* accountable for its decision. And within less than a circuit, it was obviously wanting to get back to Max. It was rewarded with pats and scratches, and then the saddle was again placed on its back. This time it let Max fasten the girth – and note that all the time Max is aware of how the horse is communicating. Often horses turn and sniff or lick the saddle, and *they should be allowed to do this* as it is their way of finding out about strange objects. If denied this opportunity they will think that there is something amiss or dangerous about this object, and instead of accepting it they will become suspicious.

The horse was then left free to experience the feel of the saddle; Max finds that most appreciate this chance to buck and let fly, and that they very quickly realise the saddle will neither hurt them nor go away. And as the experience has not been nasty, they generally accept it. But it is important that they have this time and these experiences: we cannot tell the horse that things are going to be all right and that he shouldn't worry – he has to find this out for himself. What we *can* do, however, is set up the situation so he can experience things without over-exposing himself to risk or danger.

A bridle is then placed on the horse, and Max finds that most accept this process happily if they have been properly prepared. Horses which Max starts are mouthed well in advance of the backing process, as we have seen, and young horses which have been mouthed and are used to having headcollars on therefore have little problem with a

All is well, the saddle has been fully accepted, and Max prepares to work the horse on two lines. He has the stirrups hanging down but secures them with a spare stirrup leather

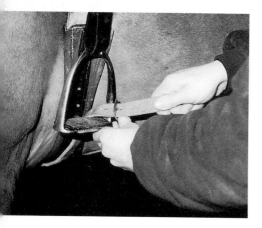

bridle. The saddle, being a much larger and heavier piece of equipment, will naturally cause the horse more concern.

The next stage is long-reining, and again, this procedure is initially carried out in the round pen. The lines are attached to the bit and fed through the stirrup irons. A stirrup leather is slipped through one iron, passed under the horse's belly, slipped through the other iron and then fastened to prevent the irons flapping around. The outside line is brought round behind the quarters. Max keeps the lines fairly loose in his hands as he does not want to catch the horse in the mouth; all he wants to do is create situations in which the horse can learn: by putting it in a situation of pressure (remember how the foal was halter broken) and letting it find its own way out of the situation, it will inevitably make decisions of its own free will.

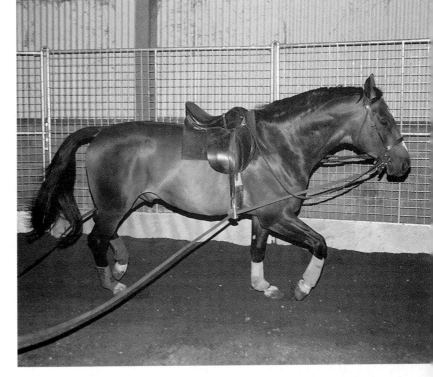

Using both lines and working in the pen, Max then starts to teach the horse to turn when asked. Horses usually find the left turn easier, so this is the one he starts with. As all horses are individuals some learn more quickly than others, as was perfectly evident in the case of two of the horses used in the demonstration evening referred to earlier. The one which looked more physically mature was not, in fact, as quick to learn the turns as the other horse, which was very sharp mentally.

If a horse is going to object to turning it is generally when he is asked to go to the right, his more difficult side. As he grows in understanding and confidence, however, you will see him moving more freely and generally being more relaxed. Once the horse is turning in each direction, Max asks for a step of rein-back before moving on to the next stage. Many people do not teach the rein-back until the horse is going forwards properly, but Max feels that this leaves the potential for the horse to take control of the situation, and to use going backwards against his rider/handler.

The stallion is worked on the two lunge lines, being asked to go forwards, to change direction, and eventually to perform a few steps of rein-back

How much time is spent with the horse at each of these stages varies with the individual; but each day's work should provide good situations from which he can learn. If you set things up badly, however, or take things too quickly, your horse will soon let you know and you will then need to go back several stages. There is no substitute for investing time in your horse – but equally it is important not to bore him to death! Remember that young minds readily soak up experiences, and need to be stimulated in the correct way.

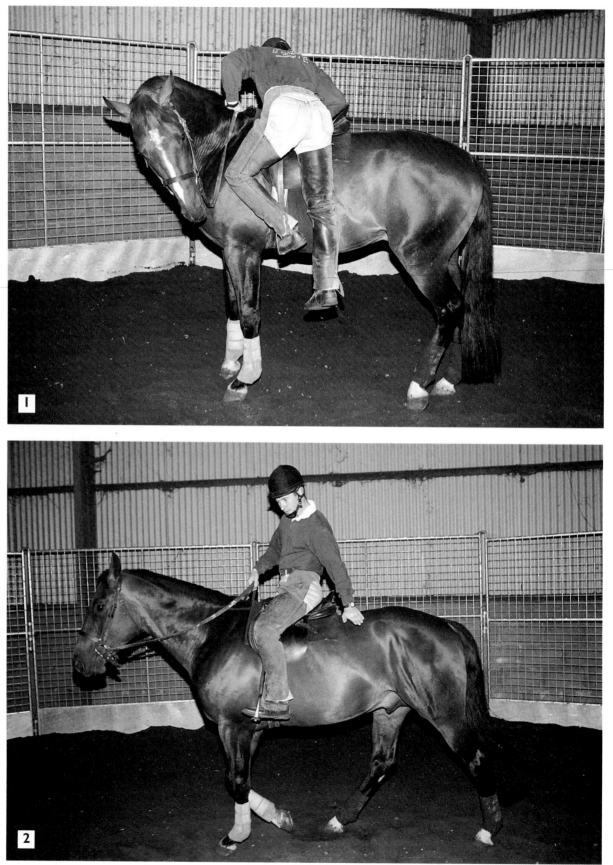

Backing

In his demonstrations on starting young horses Max reveals his whole method: the joining-up process, introducing the saddle, using two lunge lines, teaching the horse to turn and to rein back, and then his preparations for mounting; these are as follows:

- A mounting block is placed alongside the horse, first on the near side and then the offside. By standing on this, Max accustoms the horse to seeing something higher than him on both sides.
- Working on each side, he puts weight onto the saddle so that the horse feels it move on his back.
- He lies across the horse, again working from each side so the horse has a chance to overcome his instinctively fearful reaction – and instead of seeing a predator climbing on his back, he sees Max whom he can trust and relate to. During this time the horse is being subjected to conscious thought, Max's treatment provoking questions such as: 'Do I allow my instincts to take over and get rid of this thing climbing on to me?'

Basically, Max is asking the horse to believe in him and to override his instincts: 'We can only really control a horse by using his mind; it is no contest at all if you try to use your strength against a horse because you can only hold on to him for so long. The beauty of the horse is that he does give us so much. Essentially we have a

1 *Before he mounts, Max puts weight into the stirrup and lets the horse experience this feeling, as well as that of a rider leaning over his back. He will also work on his offside so that he is used to seeing something on that side of him; as we tend to do most things to our horses from the near side it can be a shock to him suddenly to see something on the offside. He is still free: no one is making him stay there with Max, it is his own conscious decision to do so. Part of the pre-mounting preparation is to let the horse see that his friend will apparently 'grow out of his back'; it can be unnerving for him to see this strange being so much higher than he is*

2 *Once on board Max walks and trots the horse around on both reins, riding positively to give him confidence. This work will be repeated over the next few days until Max feels the horse is ready to be taken outside the pen*

3 *The end of the session, and this horse is quite relaxed about the whole procedure. If a horse reacts negatively at any stage during the backing process then Max goes back a step to ensure that he is fully confident and has accepted all that has happened to him up to that point*

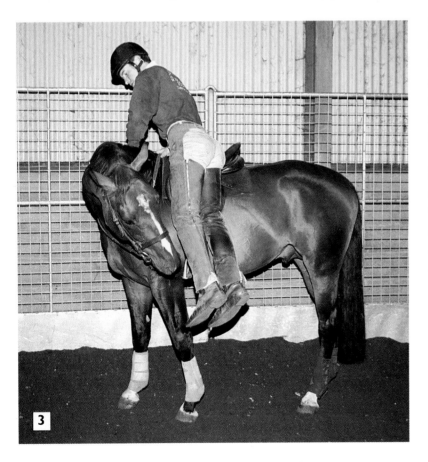

3

partnership with him – though I like to think of it as our having 51 per cent of the shares, so that we have the controlling interest!'

As long as all the groundwork has been properly done, then the horse enters into the partnership freely and the backing process is much safer for both horse and rider. Having been allowed time to buck and to express himself freely when the saddle was first placed on his back, the horse will generally accept the saddle and rider straightaway and with no fuss. 'If your horse tries to buck you off then you have made a wrong judgement and you will have to go back to basics,' says Max.

From early days teach your horse to move over and back on command

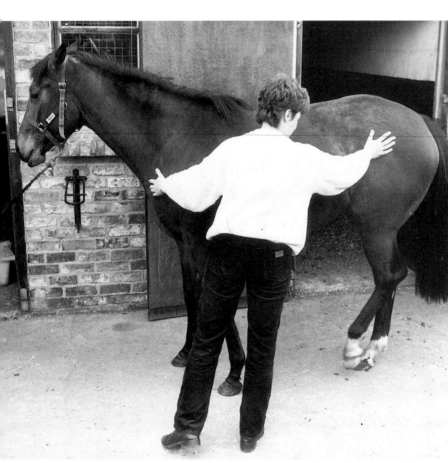

From the initial backing, Max then works in a gradually progressive way over several days until the rider is walking, trotting and cantering the horse in the pen, and also turning to left and right, and stopping. Each day the stages leading up to mounting the horse should be carried out more quickly – although always be sensitive to the signals the horse is sending. Nevertheless, the point should soon be reached where the horse is tacked up in his stable and brought into work. From then on he can be hacked out in company with other horses at first, and then on his own.

Much of the work before and after the starting process is similar to that used by 'conventional' methods of breaking horses. The huge difference with Max's method is the tremendous extent to which the horse's own psychology and methods of communication are used to benefit both horse and trainer. Moreover, once a horse has been allowed full expression in response to new experiences, has undergone conscious thought, and has fully accepted new events, then the chances of him throwing up problems later are reduced. However, if full expression is not allowed – if the horse is restrained, for example on a lunge line – then it will have been deprived of a necessary experience and the feeling of having 'missed out' will always be there, perhaps to re-surface later with, for example, a bucking bronco act when the horse decides that it wants a controlling interest in the arrangement it has with its rider.

SUMMARY

- Caring owners will want to prepare their young horse properly for life's challenges, and this includes stimulating his mind and securing his acceptance of many aspects of life, rather than just leaving him in a field for three years.

- In many respects the horse is the teacher and we have to learn from him.

- You want your horse to regard you as the good, positive thing in his life so that he trusts and believes in you to such an extent that he will over-ride his instincts, however strong these may be, in deference to your judgement.

- By letting you touch his vulnerable areas, a horse is allowing you to prove beyond all doubt that you are not going to hurt him.

- The horse's acceptance of you should be so confirmed that he will allow you to subject him to entirely new (to him) processes and experiences without any fuss at all, such as putting on tack.

- Depriving a horse of essential experiences will only lead to problems in later life.

- Allow your horse free expression – and by this we mean he should be completely unrestrained – so that he can make his own decisions.

- Always try to move around horses in a fluent, confident way. If you behave as if you expect trouble, then no doubt they will oblige!

- Your partnership should be 51 per cent you, 49 per cent the horse. Note there are some horses who will readily take control, so you must be aware of the difference between being *passive* (via your body language) but not submissive.

- Using these methods you can influence a horse's mind into accepting things.

- Horses generally do not want to be bad; they are simply following their instincts.

Horses have vulnerable areas – their neck, back, legs and belly – all places where a predator might strike and cause fatal injury. It is therefore a great measure of trust that a horse will let you pick its feet up, because in so doing it is forfeiting its ability to flee

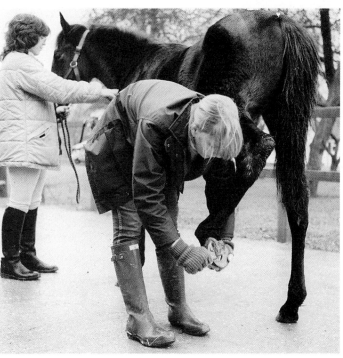

BEHAVIOURAL PROBLEMS

It is to be hoped that as a horse owner you also consider yourself to be a horse trainer: after all, it is your responsibility to ensure that your horse is well mannered, well schooled and a pleasure to own and ride. However, there is surely an element missing from this equation. You are training the horse, but shouldn't you also be training yourself? Teaching yourself to be disciplined, learning to understand more clearly how your horse thinks and sees the world, and how to communicate effectively with him?

There

are a great many people who 'train' their horses by such means as intimidation, dominance and fear. But the relationship they achieve is a long way from a true partnership with their horse. Of course, it may work for a short while, and they may even achieve some 'success' in competitions – but in the long term they have achieved nothing. In addition, they have ruined a potentially wonderful partnership with that most generous of animals, the horse.

Ideally, all horses would get the sort of start in life that Richard Maxwell offers. Unfortunately, a large number have unpleasant experiences during their lives, and these set the tone for their future behaviour. These experiences may not necessarily be inflicted on them by people who have the express purpose of making their life difficult; often these handlers are acting in what they believe is the best way for the horse, following accepted practices without questioning the reasoning behind them.

Sometimes a handler makes a mistake which he considers as just unfortunate, but without long-lasting effects – for example, perhaps he lets the lunge lines wrap themselves round a horse's legs. However, from the horse's point of view, having his legs attacked in this way is a major problem, since his prime method of survival is flight – if you deprive him of the means for that, you are putting his life at grave risk. So a seemingly innocent accident can have a considerable impact on the way a horse views you; and if he loses trust in you, it is hardly surprising if he is reluctant to let you near him again – in this example,

◄ You must have a consistent set of rules for your horse to live by: too often people encourage a youngster's playful and 'appealing' behaviour but then reprimand him when this turns more serious, for example when nipping develops into biting. This can be confusing for the horse, for you have allowed him to get away with some activities and have then suddenly turned against him. If he always knows where he stands there can be no confusion or resentment about enforcing the rules

This sort of occurrence may have a negative and long-lasting effect in the horse's mind. After such a happening you need to go back to basics and re-establish the horse's confidence in you, his handler, before you attempt long-lining again

An unhappy horse which has to undergo something of a contortion just to see out of his stable. There could be several reasons for this piece of wood across the top space, but it is questionable as to whether the horse's real problem is being addressed, or whether just the symptoms are being treated

he will understandably be wary of letting anyone handle his legs. The problem may then be further compounded by rough handling, because there are still some people who will use any means to ensure that he lets them do whatever they want with him – and if this means beating him into submission, then sadly that is what they will do.

Fortunately the number of horse owners and handlers who find this sort of dominance unappealing and unnecessary is increasing; as a consequence, they are looking for more enlightened ways of dealing with their horses. The methods which Richard Maxwell employs are based in a true assessment of equine psychology; they have lasting effects because the horse is not dictated to, but is involved in the decisions and committed to them.

When talking about problems such as cribbing or box-walking, many people refer to them as 'vices', a description also used in many books and magazines. However, the use of the word 'vice' is unfortunate because it implies that the problem is exceedingly serious and that the horse is in some way vicious; in fact, many of these problems could be avoided if the horse's natural way of life were considered by its owner or handler. As with so many aspects of dealing with horses, prevention is better than cure. Again, often the 'solutions' to problems deal with the symptoms, but ignore the cause, and therefore do nothing to ease the source of the horse's anxiety or fear. The only way he is able to convey his frustration and misery is through abnormal behaviour.

Difficulties may manifest themselves when the horse is being ridden, and/or when it is handled. A number of common problems are addressed here, with a look at some of the traditional, oft-quoted remedies, and some alternatives which Richard Maxwell has found useful.

Weaving
Symptoms

The horse rocks from one foreleg to the other, his head and neck swinging from side to side. He may behave in this way with his head and neck over the stable door, or he may stand inside the stable and carry on there. Some horses weave when standing in a lorry, and I

A grille fitted to prevent a horse weaving. However, this only treats the symptoms; it does not deal with the root cause of the problem

have even witnessed a horse weaving whilst out at grass – although this was due to severe stress because it had been bullied by another.

Why does it happen?

It is unnatural for horses to be confined within a stable for long periods, although unfortunately this is the way of life imposed upon many. Their natural behaviour is to live in the company of their own kind, roaming over large areas and grazing most of the time. When they are prevented from doing this their energies have to be used elsewhere, and some horses will start to weave. A traumatic event may also result in them displaying their anxieties or distress by weaving.

What can you do?

Give the horse more freedom: turn him out for as long as possible each day, preferably with other horses. If you can, keep the horse out. Horses are designed to live out – and furthermore, it is perfectly possible for them to be successful in competition even if they are *not* shut in.

A horse which is being bullied by another may show his distress by weaving. If this is the case, then change the living arrangements so that horses are not bullied.

If your horse has to spend most of his time in the stable, an anti-weaving grille may be fitted to the bottom half of the door. This fills the space normally occupied by the top door, with just a V-shape left in the middle through which the horse can put his head. It certainly discourages some horses from weaving, but others simply stand inside the stable and weave. You could also try hanging two plastic bottles, half filled with water, from the roof and just inside the stable; this is meant to have the same effect as the anti-weaving grille. The bottles

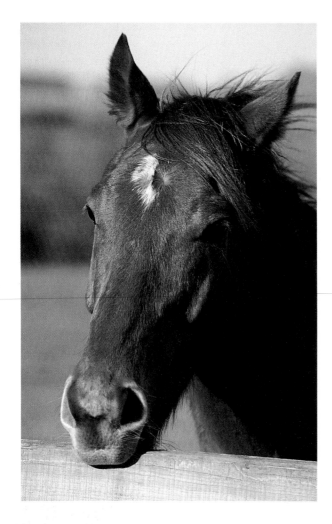

Some habits are so ingrained into the horse's behaviour that they indulge in them even when they are at liberty in the field

need to be placed so that if the horse starts to weave, he sets the bottles swinging, and in theory this discourages the activity. However, confirmed weavers just move elsewhere in the stable so they can carry on unhindered.

Try to split up your horse's day if he is stabled. Keep him interested by giving him smaller feeds more often, and provide 'toys' for him, for example the giant scented apples which are available now. Try to organise several shorter exercise periods rather than one longer one.

Sometimes a change of yard helps. Some horses weave regularly when kept in a large yard, whereas in a smaller set-up they seem to be more relaxed and weave less. It may also be that the horse only weaves when someone is in the stable; perhaps in the past he has been mistreated when stabled. Alternatively he may weave if he cannot see or hear other horses. Thus it is important to establish exactly why an animal behaves like this, particularly as it can be difficult to keep the condition on a weaver.

Many people fear that habits such as weaving will be imitated by other horses in the same yard: but horses do not necessarily learn good habits from each other, so why should they learn bad ones?

Weaving is regarded as an unsoundness and should be declared by anyone selling a horse; your vet will also record it on your pre-purchase veterinary examination certificate. An additional problem relating to weaving is that the constant rocking to and fro can place undue strain on the horse's forelegs, and bad cases may even become lame. For really confirmed weavers there is no way of stopping them: it is rather like an addiction, and a junkie will do anything to get his fix.

Cribbing and Windsucking
Symptoms

The horse takes hold of the top of the stable door, the top of a fence or any handy projection with his teeth and sucks in air: this is known as cribbing. Some horses arch their necks and swallow air without necessarily biting on to anything: these are windsuckers, and you can actually hear them gulping the air.

Because windsuckers have air present in the digestive tract their digestion of food is less efficient; this means that it is harder to keep such animals in good condition.

Two types of collar designed to prevent horses crib-biting. In order to crib-bite the horse has to arch his neck and grab hold of an object; however, when wearing either of these collars he is prevented from doing this quite so easily because they apply pressure on the neck muscles which the horse must use when he tries to crib-bite. The leather collar (shown left) has been designed by an equine dentist and is the latest device of its type on the market. The centre piece fits under the horse's jowl and makes it uncomfortable for the horse when he tries to arch his neck

Why does it happen?

It is a reaction to stress. Initially the horse may simply gnaw at the manger or parts of the stable or fencing, but then the habit develops until he is swallowing air. Insufficient roughage or bulk food combined with long periods of confinement and unsuitable management can result in this behaviour.

What can you do?

Review the horse's management, as you would for a weaver. Provide *ad lib* bulk food if the horse is stabled. However, some horses will crib and windsuck when turned out as well. It is often said that other horses will copy those with bad habits, so some yard owners are not keen to have weavers, cribbers and suchlike on their premises. However, research has been carried out which shows that they are not necessarily copied – but if an animal's circumstances encourage such a habit developing, or if it is inclined that way, then that particular behaviour pattern may well develop. It's rather like a family where the parents smoke: some of their children may follow their example, and some may not.

67

There are many preparations available which discourage horses from biting wood or grabbing hold of it in order to crib

A broad strap called a windsucking strap can be fitted to horses with this habit. Basically it fastens around the neck just where the head joins the neck, and the theory is that if it is fastened tightly enough it will prevent the muscles contracting and so help prevent windsucking. It is a form of self-punishment in that immediately the horse tries to windsuck he is uncomfortable. This device will certainly slow him down, but I have seen and heard horses windsuck whilst wearing these straps.

The stabling and fencing can be painted with bitter aloes or a similar anti-chew mixture which does seem to have a deterrent effect for cribbers. Windsuckers, however, can still continue their habit.

One further difficulty which often arises with cribbers is that their incisor teeth are damaged, with the result that they may have problems grazing properly. Check the teeth of any prospective equine purchase for uneven and excessive wear on the incisors; this is a sure sign of a cribber.

There are surgical corrections for this problem but their success rate is variable. Like weaving, it is something of an addictive habit and therefore difficult to do anything about once it is firmly established.

Kicking in the Box
Symptoms
This may take various forms: kicking the door, kicking out generally, or kicking at people.

Why does it happen?
Kicking the door is often done at mealtimes or to gain attention – and some horses just like the noise! But perhaps it may indicate that the horse is fed up, uncomfortable, hungry, frustrated or feeling lonely because he is separated from his friends.

If he kicks out a great deal when stabled it may be that he is infested with parasites, particularly if he has heavily feathered legs; or plagued with visitors such as rats or mice which use his stable as a thoroughfare. (Do remember when mucking out to move the banks of the bed each day otherwise mice will make the most of the undisturbed bedding and build their homes in it.)

A horse may kick out at people because he has been roughly handled in the past; because he has no respect for humans; or because he knows that such behaviour scares the handler and therefore gets rid of unwanted human attention. Kicking is generally a defensive rather than an aggressive action.

What can you do?
Quite apart from being annoying because of the noise, door-kicking is also potentially harmful to the horse's legs and feet owing to the constant concussion. The traditional way of dealing with this problem is to fit rubber matting or similar to the door so that when the horse

kicks, the noise is deadened somewhat and there is less of an impact on the foot. An even better method is to suspend the rubber matting so that it hangs a few inches away from the door itself, so there is a gap between the door and the matting; then when the horse kicks the mat it moves and doesn't make a noise. Since this is not as satisfying as kicking something solid which makes a good bang the horse is not achieving its objective and is likely to give up – and while it is trying out the new arrangement its feet will not suffer, either.

If parasites are the problem, consult your vet for the appropriate treatment; but ensure that in the future your horse is kept clean and well groomed. Vermin problems need to be addressed: your local authority can advise on measures if the numbers are large; or alternatively poison can be put down along the routes taken by mice and rats. Poison should always be carefully placed so that stable cats and dogs do not accidentally eat it.

Kicking out at people is a habit which needs careful assessment. Why, exactly, does the horse do it? And when does he do it? Horses are very good at training us not to do things that they do not like or are unsure about; for instance, those which are particularly ticklish are good at pulling faces, swishing tails or threatening to kick at the people who try to groom them – and very often they get the result they want, for the person backs off and only carries out the undesirable task when really necessary. Instead, what we should do is carry it out so often that the horse becomes thoroughly bored with making such a fuss and no longer acts in a naughty or aggressive way.

The way in which you deal with the horse during this transitional period is very important. As regards the kicking problem, try creating a situation where the horse is responsible for its own actions. One solution Max devised himself is to fit up a bangle with bored-out ball bearings, and then to fit it around the pastern; if the horse kicks out, the bangle whacks down on the coronary band and so the horse effectively punishes itself for its bad behaviour.

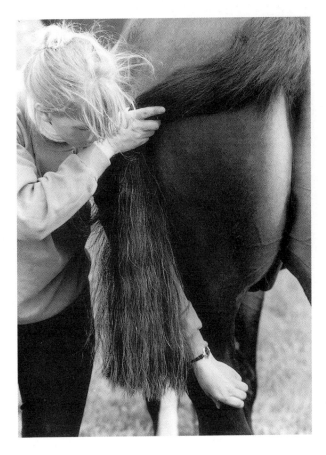

A simple measure such as holding the tail to the side is said to be a preventive measure against a horse kicking out; a serious kicker will not subscribe to this view, however!

Box-walking
Symptoms

The horse walks constantly round its stable, hardly ever standing still. Often this 'walking' is carried out at great speed with the horse seemingly unaware of anyone who happens to be in the way.

Why does it happen?

For some reason the horse is extremely unhappy. The obvious answer is that he does not like being confined in the stable – but horses are quite capable of jumping out of stables, and the problem can also be seen in animals out at pasture when they will pace up and down near the gate. It is essential that the owner or handler finds out the reason for the horse's unhappy state of mind.

What can you do?

The horse can be prevented from walking round his box by using such tactics as placing car tyres on the floor; he then has to slow down and pick his way round them. Alternatively, empty feed bags can be hung from the ceiling, again to hamper his progress around the box. Both these methods are devised so as to make box-walking so awkward for the horse that he chooses the easy way out of the situation and stands still. However, it must be remembered that the horse started box-walking as a way of coping with some other problem that was distressing him, and if not allowed to release his anxiety in this way he might well turn to other 'vices' such as weaving to release his frustration.

It is therefore vital that the root cause of the problem is found. Many problems arise because the horse is in pain, but the whole of his lifestyle and behaviour need to be examined in order to pinpoint the problem area. Once the root cause has been addressed, the box-walking will either stop or be alleviated.

A horse in Max's 'bag box', where empty feed sacks are suspended from the ceiling. This is used for horses which are headshy or generally rather flighty. The horse has to move around the box amongst all the bags to reach his feed and water, and so comes to terms with his aversion

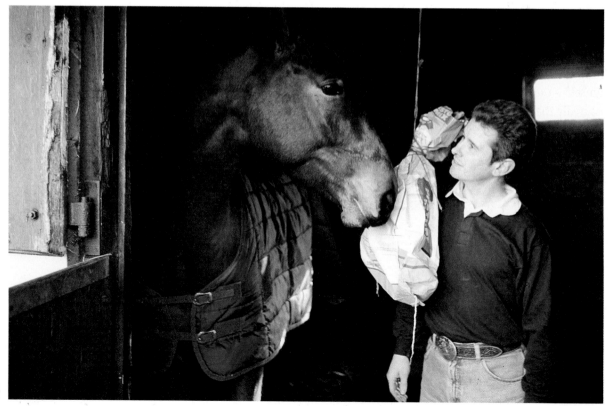

Bully in the Stable
Symptoms

The horse may bite or snap at anyone who comes near or into his stable; he may kick out, lunge, turn his hindquarters to face you and threaten to kick. He may also try to squash you.

Why does it happen?

Bearing in mind that horses are basically nervous, cowardly creatures, there has to be a reason for them apparently turning into bullies! It is often the case that horses categorised as vicious and aggressive by their owners or handlers are in fact just the opposite: in other words they are nervous and insecure but their dealings with humans have resulted in them developing this sort of behaviour as a system of self-defence.

If a horse has been subjected to aggressive, abusive handling from humans then he will react to violence with violence. This is instinctive: if he feels threatened and is unable to flee, he will fight with teeth and hooves. Before resorting to this sort of aggressive behaviour the horse does, however, put out messages warning of his impending action. You have probably seen horses having a disagreement in the field: say horse A tries to pinch some of B's hay; B will squeal, lay his ears back and turn his quarters to A, at which point A may back off. If A doesn't, then B may lift a leg to warn that a kick will follow. Should A still not take the hint, then B will have to resort to the final defence of kicking.

Throughout this dispute the communication between both horses has been quite clear, and you have probably seen horses behave in this way towards humans; and it is a sad fact that some owners are quite used to being greeted by their horse's hindquarters when they go into the stable. Do *not*, however, dismiss this as your horse just 'being himself' – that is, miserable: there has to be a reason for it, and just as assuredly there is a way in which you can overcome it. Thus biting and snapping may be caused by rough handling, for example when grooming, or perhaps by doing up the girth too quickly and too tightly; by feeding titbits (not a practice to be recommended, because some horses become very pushy and cross once the titbits are no longer forthcoming; your horse's best reward should be a pat or stroke from you); or by mismanagement – the horse was perhaps the victim of aggressive, violent treatment at the hands of previous owners.

What can you do?

With a horse that tries to squash you, the worst thing you can do is try to push him off you, because a horse will lean into pressure rather than move away from it (which it must be trained to do). Therefore the more you lean against him the more he will lean against (and squash) you. The most effective thing you can do is to poke him repeatedly in the ribs or belly with your fingers or knuckles, making your jabs at him short and sharp. Horses do not like this and will quickly move away

A clear demonstration of the fact that a horse is an interpressure animal: the more Max leans into this pony, the more the pony leans into him. This is why it is no use trying to use your strength to push away a horse which is squashing you against a wall!

(think how promptly a horse learns to move away from you if you jab him in the side with your foot every time you mount).

Learn to reprimand a horse in the way that another horse would: thus pushing him away or giving him a sharp nudge in the neck would be seen as a telling-off; whereas raising your hand and hitting him, particularly about the head, or whacking him with a stick, would be considered an act of aggression and you would be categorised immediately as a predator, reinforcing the horse's impression that you should be warned off.

One way to get a horse to move away from you is by jabbing him with your finger; short, sharp jabs are most effective

Biting or snapping when he is groomed is probably because he doesn't like you intruding on his personal space or his vulnerable areas (his belly or his head). However, grooming is a natural procedure which horses enjoy administering to each other, and there is no reason why yours should not be happy to allow you to groom it. If, however, you back off when it snaps at you, then you are letting the horse make the choice about when or whether you touch it. Instead you should stand firm and insist, nicely, that the horse lets you into those vulnerable areas. Say you have a ticklish, rather crotchety mare: handle her several times a day, and show her you are not going to let her escape your attentions by placing the palm of one hand firmly on her belly whilst keeping the other hand on her back. Speak to her reassuringly, and do *not* snatch your hand away if she threatens to kick or bite. Keep your hand still and firm: she has to learn that the only way to get rid of you is to behave. Do this regularly whilst you are grooming her, gradually asking a little more each time so that you progress to patting and stroking her belly before taking your hand away. Eventually you should be able to use a cloth, and then a brush instead of your hand, and can then groom her properly – and she may even come to enjoy it!

Stamping and Pawing
Why does it happen?

The horse may just like to hear the noise; it may be frustrated or anxious, or it may be exploring or testing out its surroundings (especially a young horse in a new environment); it may be impatient, for example if about to be fed, or if its friend has gone out to grass before it; or it could be a sign of pain, such as colic.

What can you do?
Remove the cause if the problem can be attributed to pain, frustration or anxiety. Ensure the horse has a deep bed so as to minimise damage to the legs should it persist in the habit.

If its bed has been unduly disturbed you should look out for indications of other problems: for example it may be in pain because of colic, or be uncomfortable for some reason, perhaps because its rugs have slipped, or because it has been cast (check for scrape marks on the stable walls and for injuries on the horse's legs and sides); it is disturbed by rats; it feels unhappy because it is kept on its own, or alternatively because it is being bullied; it feels restless because of insufficient exercise. Note that horses will often play with new bedding.

Refusal to Lie Down
Why does this happen?

The horse may be anxious if he is in new surroundings; he may be stabled next to a horse which has bullied him and he therefore feels anxious; he might have unhappy memories of being cast; he may have slipped when getting up and so is reluctant to lie down again.

What can you do?
Determine the reason for the problem and act accordingly. Ensure the bed is deep enough, with good banks. Try different beds – rubber, shavings, paper – in different stables if possible. Give the horse long steady work for a few days to encourage him to lie down and rest.

Plastic or leather muzzles may slow down a horse which eats his bed, but you should try to work out why he has developed the habit in the first place. Is he bored, perhaps; or does he have digestive problems?

If bed-eating is a habit with your horse, do be careful in your choice of bedding. Some horses find hemp beddings palatable, for example, while others will gorge on straw (particularly oat straw). Such habits may result in colic. If your stable has a sloping floor which drains well, consider investing in rubber bedding – it is cost-effective, safe and labour-saving.

Eating Bedding
Why does it happen?

This problem may arise because the horse is bored, or because he has not been provided with sufficient bulk food.

What can you do?
Ensure the horse's diet is balanced and meets his requirements.

If you have to bed the horse on straw a muzzle can be used, once he has eaten his night-time hay ration. These muzzles are like a small bucket with holes in the sides, held on to the horse's muzzle by way of a strap which fits over his head behind the ears. He can drink, but is not meant to be able to eat – although horses have been known to pile all their bedding up and then plunge their head into the heap so that bits of straw go down the muzzle.

Alternatively you could change to a non-edible bedding such as paper or shavings. Should the horse continue to eat his bedding, and if he chews his stable excessively, then consult your vet because there may be a severe digestive problem.

If boredom is the cause, then the horse's daily routine and management must be reviewed (*see* Weaving).

Ripping and Tearing of Rugs and Bandages
Why does it happen?
Colts will often pull and tear at rugs; either the rugs smell new or of other horses, and the colt wants them to smell of him so he tries to get them off in order to 'mark' them with his own smell. Youngsters generally, and colts in particular, do also tend to explore things with their teeth; this is natural behaviour. And when teething, youngsters do chew things.

There may, of course, be other reasons why horses rip their rugs and try to get them off, for example if they are too hot, or if the rug is causing them to itch (some washing powders cause an allergic reaction). Boredom could also be a factor.

What can you do?
There are some foul-tasting preparations available such as bitter aloes which can be painted onto rugs. Also it is important to ensure that a rug fits the horse properly; if it doesn't, you can hardly blame him for wanting to get rid of it. And avoid putting rugs down on bedding as the bits of straw or shavings which will catch onto the underside could irritate the horse's skin.

Refusing to Back or Move Over

A horse should be taught to back and to move over on command; in the stable this has obvious uses: he can then be moved back easily from the stable door when you want to come in; he can be moved to either side without hassle, for example if you are mucking out and he is still in the box (when he should always be tied up), or when you want to put boots on and are generally working around him. Teaching your horse to move backwards and sideways on command is also useful as a preparation for ridden work: thus he will understand more readily what you want if the rein-back lesson can be accompanied by a vocal request to back. Also, teaching the horse to move sideways in response to pressure on the girth area is an effective early instruction to lateral work.

To teach a horse to back, stand to one side of him and first make sure that his head is down rather than stuck up in the air: to encourage him to drop his head, stroke both his ears, working from the base towards the tips and using long, firm strokes. This helps to relax him and will persuade him to lower his head. Then push him firmly in the chest whilst at the same time giving him the verbal command 'back'. You must always ensure first of all that he has enough room actually to take a step or two backwards. As soon as he responds, cease pushing, praise him, and end the session for the time being. Repeat the same lesson later: frequent short periods, where you make it easy for the horse to understand so he is almost bound to respond in the way you

Young horses and ponies are curious and will tend to explore things with their mouths – so think carefully before you leave anything valuable within reach of a youngster!

75

Narrow doorways such as this can create problems, because if the pony bangs his hip on the door frame as he goes through he will be quite justified in not wanting to walk through it again – and of course, horses have long memories for such experiences. The steps down could also cause it to jar itself. Sometimes it is a simple occurrence such as this which causes the pony to behave in the way it does, because of the discomfort it is made to suffer

want, will result in a movement quickly and thoroughly learnt.

If the horse does not take a step back when asked, you might exert extra pressure by tapping the coronet of the hoof closest to you, using just the toe of your boot. When he raises his leg, push him again in the chest, simultaneously saying 'back'.

If your horse still refuses to co-operate, take the lead rope and place it across his muzzle, halfway between his eyes and nostrils. Pull it gently back and forth in a sawing motion and ask him again to 'go back' – this usually works, though do bear in mind that this is a very sensitive area of the horse's face and so do *not* use too great a pressure.

Some horses may have a physical problem which makes it uncomfortable for them to back, and they will therefore resist any attempts to make them do so; it is their way of telling you that something is wrong. With such cases it is important that you consult your vet and get to the root of their trouble. Note, too, *how* the horse moves backwards: it should move its legs in diagonal pairs, but if it shows any marked irregularity in its way of stepping, a veterinary opinion should be sought.

Difficult to Lead

Some horses barge in and out of their stable, others cart their owners around when being led to the field, yet others are generally bolshy all the time. The end result is that both horse and handler are in danger of being injured, as are other parties.

There are many reasons why a horse might barge around. For instance, if he banged his hips whilst being led into or out of a stable,

Wrapping the lead-rope around its nose is a common way of dealing with an animal which pulls when being led. However, if all horses were properly halter-broken as foals, then every single one would be a pleasure to lead!

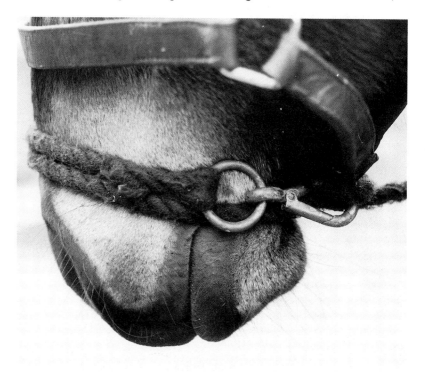

If your horse has been properly halter-broken he will know that when pressure is applied he must step forwards towards his handler in order to remove the pressure, make life more comfortable and gain a reward in the form of a pat. During this training the horse learns to watch the lead-rope: when it is tight, life becomes uncomfortable. He soon learns not to fight, to move when the handler moves, and to stand when the handler stands. The horse can also be taught to back up when the rope is wiggled

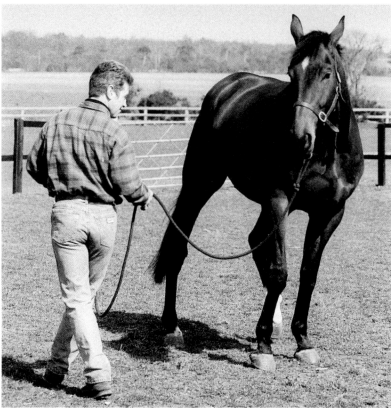

You can see here how the horse is watching Max and is already preparing to follow him. Notice

how slack the lead-rope is

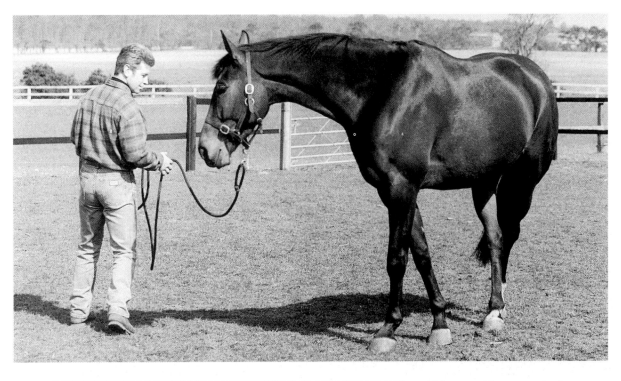

Wherever Max goes the horse follows. Notice how different this turn is compared to the next picture, which shows the way most of us are taught to handle horses

It is common practice for a handler to grasp hold of the horse's head and restrain it fiercely, rather than just letting the horse be there (as in the previous picture)

then understandably he will be tempted to rush on subsequent occasions, his instinctive reaction being to hurry past anything threatening. Or it might be the memory of a bad experience, or pain; or sheer bolshiness could be the cause. How you handle the individual horse therefore differs according to the root cause: firmness is needed for the bolshy ones, whereas patient cajolery will play a greater part in the encouragement of the more frightened, and it is up to each owner to identify the motivating circumstances for the horse's behaviour.

Remember that horses instinctively dislike narrow, dark spaces: their sense of survival warns them that danger may be lurking there. Yet we ask them, and expect them not to question us, to go into dark stables and travel in strange boxes on wheels. Stable doors should be 8ft high and 4ft wide (2.5 x 1.25m) and when leading in and out, take care to go through the centre of the opening and to allow room if turning for the whole of the horse's body to negotiate the opening. For a horse which barges in and/or out of his stable fit a removable bar (a piece of wood and a couple of brackets) just inside the door, across the opening at chest height. The door can then be opened safely without the horse barging through; remove the bar, and let him through calmly.

Use a bridle to give you added control, and remember to wear gloves. Be confident, and talk to the horse in a soothing voice. If he

In this situation it is quite likely that the horse will break away from its handler. However, as the next sequence of pictures shows, it is possible to prevent the horse getting the better of you

The first thing to do when dealing with a horse which is pulling away from you is to move quickly so that you are at a 45° angle to it.

From this position you can more easily unbalance it, and thus pull it round to you.

It is important then to give immediately with the long rope, and so reward the horse for moving towards you: in this way he will learn that being with you is a good experience

WARNING

Halters or devices which apply pressure to the horse's poll must be used very tactfully as this is a sensitive area of the animal and damage could easily be caused. Commercially available restrainer headcollars do not always come with instructions, so you should contact the manufacturers for additional information.

Notice how close the handler is in this situation, and how he is having to use a great deal of force

tries to barge off, use whatever word he associates with slowing down (for instance if you use 'whoa' when lungeing him, use 'whoa' now). Use your elbow in his chest as well, or tap him on the chest with a stick if necessary. Do this each time he rushes, but do *not* jab him in the mouth with the reins as this will only cause him pain and will reaffirm his conviction that going through the stable door hurts! Shouting at him or slapping him on the nose is not to be recommended: quiet, confident, firm handling is the way forwards.

If the horse is worried because on a previous occasion he has hit his head on the top of the stable door, then give him food to ensure he lowers it as he goes through the doorway.

There are a number of 'restrainer' headcollars on the market now which offer greater control for handlers.

Horses which take off and lead their owners, instead of vice versa, need speedy discipline. Use a much longer lead-rope than normal, and it is advisable to wear gloves and non-slip boots. When the horse starts to take off, immediately position yourself so that you are at 45° to his head; this gives you much greater leverage to exert a pull and anchor yourself. Providing the horse has already been properly halter-broken, once the pressure is on, he will move towards it, as this is the most comfortable position for him.

A potential hazard with the conventional method of leading is that as the handler is so close to the horse's front he is in a vulnerable position if it suddenly leaps forwards

Bolting their Feed
Symptoms

Instead of eating in a relaxed way, some horses do bolt their feed. This may be due to greed, hunger, pain or anxiety.

What can you do?

Establish the cause of the problem and act upon it. Horses can be discouraged from eating too greedily by using chaffs to bulk out the feed; by placing lumps of rock salt or mineral licks, or large, smooth stones in the feed bowl so that he has to search around these for his food (these must be so large that it is impossible for him to swallow them); by dividing the feed bowl into compartments so he cannot grab large mouthfuls. It is good practice to accustom your horse to eating a small amount of hay before his concentrate ration is provided; this activates the digestive juices and takes the edge off his appetite, which is useful with a greedy horse. Hungry horses should have their stable routine examined to ensure that they are not left for long periods without food. The horse's digestive system is designed to allow virtually continuous feeding; as a general rule, horses are grazing for around sixteen hours out of every twenty-four, and if the digestive system goes for longer than eight hours without food then it starts to break down.

83

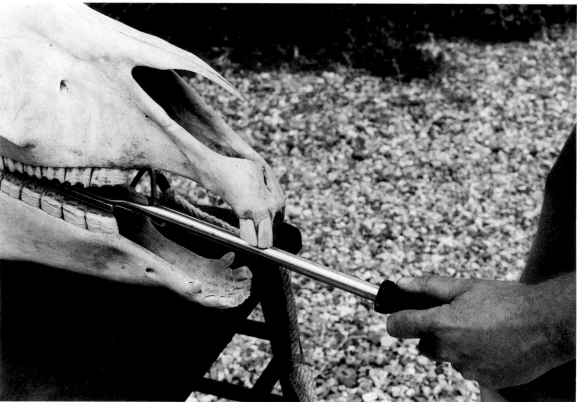

Remember the golden rule of feeding, to feed little and often in imitation of nature.

When planning your horse's feeding programme, try therefore to leave no more than five hours between his feeds. Split up his concentrate feeds into more, smaller feeds rather than one large one, and always give the largest amount of bulk food (hay) at night to keep him occupied. Use smaller-holed haynets or one net inside another to make it more time-consuming for the horse to extract the hay from the net.

Remember also one of the other essential rules of feeding: do not work a horse for at least an hour after he has finished his feed. Leave a longer gap if his exercise is to include fast work.

If a horse comes to you in a poor condition, do not try to fatten him up too quickly; any weight gain should be over a period of time in order to avoid problems.

Some horses find eating difficult because of tooth problems. As a general rule a horse's teeth should be examined and rasped at least once a year, and more frequently if he is old or is experiencing trouble. The molars and premolars in the upper jaw are set wider apart than those in the lower jaw, so when the horse grinds his food, sharp ridges develop on the outside edge of the upper teeth and inside edge of the lower molars and premolars. These edges need to be rasped so that the surfaces are smooth again; if this is not done, ulcers may develop and great soreness will result.

Tell-tale signs of tooth problems are when partially masticated mouthfuls of food drop from the jaws, indicating an apparent inability to chew it properly (known as quidding); loss of condition; eating more slowly than usual; and resentment when being bridled, or if asked to work 'on the bit'. If a horse's teeth are really sharp the uneven edges can often be felt if you run your fingers along his face, above where the molars lie. To check inside the jaw, take hold of his tongue through the interdental space at one side of the mouth, then insert your thumb into the opposite side of his mouth and run it along his teeth.

Good equine dentists are in short supply: try to find one by word-of-mouth recommendation. Check on how good a job he is doing by making sure that he lets you feel the horse's teeth before and after he has worked on them; if the teeth surfaces are not smooth then he has not done his job properly. He will need to use a gag in order to gain access to the molars at the rear of the horse's mouth, and be suspicious if he considers he can do a good job without using such equipment.

Another reason why a horse may bolt his feed is anxiety, particularly if he is stabled next to a horse which bullies him. If this is the case, then remove the cause. Some horses do not like humans fussing around them when they are eating – how would *you* like someone trying to swop your shirt or jacket for another when you were

You can see from the horse's skull how far back the molars are in the jaw. An equine dentist would need to use a gag to be able to rasp the molars right at the back of the jaw.

PECKING ORDER

Observe horses, both in the stable and out in the field, so that you know the pecking order amongst your particular animals. This could have a direct relevance on other areas. Thus horse which is anxious about a neighbouring horse, for instance, will be even more stressed if stabled in a box with bars for the top half of the walls because a bully can intimidate another horse through the bars. This may make life miserable for the bullied animal, particularly at feed times.

trying to eat dinner? Arrange your horsey jobs to show consideration
for his needs, even if the time you can spend on them is limited.

Difficult to Catch

One of the most frustrating problems for any owner, and especially a
busy working one, is the horse which will not be caught. Having owned
a couple of these tricky characters and tried various suggestions, I have
found that the most successful and enduring solution is to 'walk the
horse down'.

Basically, you need to set aside the whole day to do this. Assuming
that the horse is already out at grass, go into the field as normal and
attempt to catch it as you normally do. When it moves away from you,
follow it – don't chase it, but don't let it settle down to graze; keep it
moving so that instead of having a leisurely day in the field eating to its
heart's content, it is having to focus on *you*. Some horses give in fairly
quickly, not appreciating the new 'game' which their owner is imposing
on them. Others, like my mare, kept on the move for some hours.
Eventually she came towards me and stood quite still while I put the
headcollar on, made a fuss of her – and then let her go again. I then
went out of the field for half an hour, returned and tried to catch her
again. She resisted for ten minutes and then gave in. On most occasions
now she will let me walk straight up to her and catch her; sometimes
she walks off, but I follow and within five minutes she has given in.

Before walking her down in this manner I had tried all sorts of
ploys: enticing her with food; removing all the other horses from the
field so that she was left alone (unfortunately she seemed to like her
'splendid isolation'); sitting in the field and ignoring her, hoping that
she would become interested and visit me (especially as I had a rustly
bag of goodies); getting together with other people to try and herd her
towards the field gate and then into an enclosed area; visiting her
regularly just to fuss her but without removing her from the field to
work. However, none of these had any enduring effect; they worked
once or twice but I had to keep changing tactics.

The important thing to remember once you have caught your
horse is to make a fuss of it, even though your feelings towards it are
not necessarily charitable! If you succeed in catching your horse but
then abuse it you will only compound the problem.

Climbing over the Stable Door

As a young child attending Pony Club camp for the first time I was
amazed to see a pony try to jump out over its stable door; it got its front
legs stuck and cut them quite badly, but apparently did this regularly.
Clearly it really disliked being stabled – maybe it was claustrophobic –
and would have been much happier living out at grass or, if it had to
come in, in a crew yard with some sort of shelter against really bad
weather.

Some animals may try to climb over the stable door but only in certain circumstances; for instance, many horses become extremely excited if the local Hunt passes close by. One horse we knew leapt out of its box and tried to follow the Hunt but ended up careering down a dual carriageway, fortunately without injury to horse, people or cars; but it could quite easily have been a disastrous tale. If a horse does get excited and tries to jump out when the Hunt is around, the best policy may be to shut its top stable door until things have quietened down (which hopefully will be in just a short while).

Jumping out at other times can be dealt with by removing the cause of the problem if possible. Another alternative is to fix a grille so that it fills the space left by the top door. If your horse is a persistent offender it may be that he suffers from claustrophobia and would be happier if he lived out all the time or in a crew yard.

Afraid of Being Clipped

Unfortunately many horses are given a bad experience when being clipped, and naturally this makes them wary and resentful of any future clipping operation. And if measures are taken to force them to succumb – being twitched or restrained in other ways – then their fear of clipping increases.

Sometimes an operator may unwittingly 'abuse' the horse when clipping: for instance the clipper blades may become very hot, or he may nick the horse's skin, an easy thing to do. Whilst the intention was not to hurt the horse in any way, all *he* knows is that clipping has caused him discomfort or even pain. And matters may also have been made worse if the horse was told off when he moved away. Imagine this scenario, which is far from uncommon: a woman unwittingly creates discomfort for her horse, who is normally good to clip, because the blades are too hot. When he moves away, she jerks on the headcollar and gives him a slap – after all, he should stand perfectly still, he's quite used to being clipped, so what is his problem? She sees no reason why he should move away and considers he is just being naughty, so reprimands him. The horse, however, has suffered discomfort from the hot blades, but when he said so (by moving away) he was immediately told off: thus his owner, whom he should be able to trust, has turned against him without reason.

Having witnessed this sort of situation on many occasions, it's no wonder that horses end up pretty confused. But the sad thing is that the person doing the clipping probably never realises that he or she is in the wrong.

Next time you clip your horse, be aware at all times of exactly what is happening: set up the situation so that the horse is not abused, and listen to what his actions are saying to you. If all horses were introduced to clipping in a sensible way, many of the problems we encounter would disappear. In fact, if you think about it, it is quite

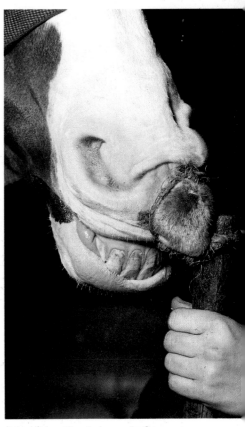

A 'traditional' twitch made from rope or twine attached to a length of wood. Applying a twitch to the nose area as shown results in the release of endorphins into the horse's body which effectively act as a sedative

CLIPPING PRECAUTIONS...

There are obvious precautions to take to ensure that you do not give your horse reason to be afraid of clipping. For instance:

- Ensure the blades are sharp.
- Have a spare set of blades to hand if the horse has a particularly heavy coat.
- Check the blades regularly to ensure they are not getting too hot.
- Service the clippers regularly, for your own safety and that of your horse.
- Don't clip a horse which is damp or dirty; you are only making a more difficult job for yourself, and there is an increased risk of nicking the horse's skin or pulling his coat around.
- Don't push the clippers too hard against the coat.
- Ensure the clippers are earthed properly: circuit breakers are inexpensive and essential.
- Arrange for the horse to be held by someone he trusts, and talk to him in a soothing way throughout the clipping operation.
- Don't let an inexperienced or careless person clip a horse which is nervous or which has never been clipped before. A nervous horse is likely to be made more nervous, and it is essential that a horse new to the experience has a pleasant introduction to set him up for hassle-free clipping sessions in the future.
- Be sensible about where you use the clippers. Many horses object to having their heads clipped, and the vibration of a full-size clipper head on their bony skull must indeed be horrendous; so consider using battery-operated clippers. Take into account, too, your horse's normal behaviour: thus a headshy horse is unlikely to take kindly to being clipped around the head.
- Make sure you have an assistant when clipping; it helps if he or she can pull the horse's front legs forwards so that you can clip around the elbow area.
- Have everything you need to hand so that you are not wasting time.
- As you remove the horse's coat, have a rug ready to put over him to keep him warm.
- If the noise of the clippers obviously upsets your horse, try de-sensitising him by playing him a tape recording of the noise for several days before he is due to be clipped.
- Plugging his ears with cotton wool will also help to deaden the noise.
- Have a radio playing – make sure it is soothing music – as this sometimes helps to calm horses during clipping.
- Seek the help of someone who is really experienced if you are unable to clip the horse yourself – and by experienced I mean someone who has to clip dozens of horses in a season, not the person who does just a couple, and quiet, well behaved ones at that!
- Do not let anyone resort to hitting your horse; if he is really objectionable, then seek the help of your vet who can sedate him. If sedation is necessary, think carefully about how many times you have him clipped during winter; sedation can prove costly, so many people try to prevent the horse's winter coat from growing too thickly by rugging him up earlier than usual.
- If you decide you will have to twitch your horse, first try gripping his top lip just with your fingers. This has the same effect as twitching and is often easier to apply to a worried horse than a twitch. You must not loosen your grip, however, and you will find it can only be held for a couple of minutes; so whoever is doing the clipping must be warned when you need to release it.
- Humane twitches are available, again to be used on the horse's top lip. Do not allow anyone to apply an ear twitch to your horse as this is cruel.
- Hand-operated clippers are also available, but in practical terms it is really only possible to execute a limited clip, for example take off the underside of the neck – unless, of course, you have hours to spare!
- Max schools horses which are difficult to clip so that they understand the 'come-along' halter: that is, if the rope is slack there is no pressure on the horse; but if he pulls away then pressure is exerted and he is uncomfortable. The horse must therefore make the right decision and come forwards so as to ease the pressure. Once a horse understands this he is then clipped – and most soon realise that even if they are silly and put themselves into an uncomfortable position the clipping will still continue.

This is known as a 'humane twitch' and is often employed to quieten horses whilst certain procedures are carried out, for example clipping

remarkable that they let us put a vibrating noisy machine, with a great long lead attached, on their bodies at all, their natural instinct being to get rid of this alien pressure as soon as possible. It is only by showing them in a kind and sympathetic way that the 'alien' will not hurt them, and by 'de-sensitising' them to it, that we have any hope of producing horses which don't object to being clipped. If they trust us and let us clip them, and then we hurt them, albeit unwittingly, it's easy to see why they are less trustful the next time. Wouldn't you be the same?

Refusing to Eat or Drink

With a new horse you should straightaway spend time getting to know it, and all its little habits: in and out of the stable, when travelling, when being tacked up and so on. By doing this you will then know if anything is out of the ordinary. Sometimes it is only a small thing which is not quite normal behaviour for the horse, but this tiny sign can be early warning of a more major problem. A common indication that something is amiss is a lack of interest in food or drink, and this

HEALTH CHECK...

- Are the horse's vital signs (temperature, pulse and respiration) normal? The normal rates are: temperature 37° to 38°C (99° to 100.5°F); pulse 30 – 42 beats per minute; and respiration 8 – 15 breaths per minute.
- Is the coat dull and rough-looking?
- Does the skin move easily? Check for dehydration by pinching a fold of skin on the neck; if it stays pinched up rather than returning to normal, then the horse is dehydrated.
- Are the droppings the normal colour and number?
- Is the urine the usual colour, and is it being passed? Check your horse when you hear it staling.
- Is the horse's bed different in any way to normal? Is it unduly disturbed, for example, perhaps indicating that a horse has been pacing around or rolling?

may vary from refusing completely to touch anything, or simply not finishing meals or not drinking as much as usual. If you observe this, then do check for other signs of health.

Have you checked...?

If all seems well with the horse, then check other factors:

- Are his feed and water bowls clean? Imagine having to eat off a plate which hasn't been washed all week! Treat your horse's eating and drinking utensils as carefully as you would your own.
- If the horse has moved to a stable with a different system – for example, automatic watering – he may not like to drink; for instance, the noise of it refilling can put some horses off.
- Have the containers been cleaned in something which has a strong smell and is off-putting to the animal?
- Moving to a new location may mean that the water tastes and smells different, so the horse may not want to drink. When going away to competitions it is sensible to take your own water supplies – and some 'home' water can also be taken to a new area in order to mix with the 'new' water if you know your horse is fussy.
- When letting your horse drink, for example at competitions and other occasions when you are watering him in hand, remember that when drinking of his own accord, the horse tends to drink, then have a short rest before drinking again. So beware of taking him away from the water source before he has properly finished.
- If the horse is living out, then perhaps the approach to the water trough/source is slippery or poached and the animal is worried about drinking.
- If the field trough is placed too close to the fence, then the horse may have fallen or become trapped and so be wary of going there again.
- Consider the pecking order in the field as well: those horses lower down the hierarchy may be prevented from drinking their fill by a bully.
- Unfortunately some horses are good at getting droppings into their water and feed bowls, and the lingering smell may put them off. If you find droppings in your horse's bowls, clean them out using a mild sterilising fluid such as one used for infant care.
- Maybe it is excitement which is causing your horse's unwillingness to drink or eat. For instance, if the local Hunt has been in the area it can take some time before the non-participating horses settle down again. Once they have calmed down they generally drink.
- Endurance horses need to drink regularly when competing, and their riders often tempt them with the water in which molassed sugar beet has been soaked.
- Sugar-beet water is worth trying if your horse is very tired and is refusing to drink. If, however, you are unable to persuade your horse to drink and he is dehydrated, do contact your vet who can get fluids into the animal and give you further help.

- If your horse will not eat, then check the quality of the feed you are giving him. Is the hay mouldy or dusty? Is the feed old? (Check the sell-by dates on bags of feed when you get them from your merchant.) Does the feed smell fine to you? Or can you detect that something is off? If haylage is being fed, remember that it must be used up within a limited time of the bag being opened; scrawl the day of opening on the bag if necessary so that you remember. If haylages smell vinegary do not use them.

- Occasionally a bag of feed may be off, so if your horse refuses to eat just after a new bag of feed has been opened, check it out!

- The horse may simply not like the feed he is being offered; it seems that some horses do go 'off' certain feeds after a time, so give them something different (remembering always to make any changes in diet gradually).

- Your expensive feed may have become contaminated by vermin, so store it in metal bins if possible, or plastic dustbins.

Eating Droppings

Known officially as *coprophagia*, this undesirable habit may occur because of a lack of bulk food, boredom, insufficient mineral salts or worm infestation.

Do not be alarmed if you see young foals eating their dams' droppings for it is a means by which they build up their gut bacteria. Older horses which have recently received antibiotics may display the habit as their gut bacteria could have been depleted by the medication.

Ask an equine nutritionist to check your horse's diet for you in order to identify any dietary deficiency which can then be rectified. Feed manufacturers do employ nutritionists and run helplines providing free advice, so make use of these services. In order to give you a considered opinion the nutritionist will need to know the following details:

1 Your horse's bodyweight.
2 How much feed (in weight, not scoops) he is currently getting, and what type.
3 Your horse's age, breed and type; for example, is he a good doer, or a fussy eater?
4 Your horse's daily workload.
5 His time out at grass and the quality of the grazing.
Have this information to hand when you call for help.

If boredom is contributing to the habit, then change your horse's day to make life more interesting: for example, turn him out if he is currently stabled for long periods; find him an amicable equine companion if he is normally kept alone (which is not advisable as horses are gregarious and need the company of their own kind – alternative company, even

WHAT YOU CAN DO

Determine the cause of the problem and resolve it:

- Even horses in hard work should receive a minimum of 25 per cent of their total daily feed as bulk food, for example hay, haylage.

- Implement a regular worming programme: every four to six weeks in the summer, every six to eight weeks in winter. Remember to double dose (but consult your vet first) against tapeworm at least once a year (July) and preferably twice (July and October); to treat for bots in November/ December; and to worm against encysted small redworm in November.

- Supply a vitamin and mineral lick in the field and stable.

a sheep, is better than nothing at all); split up his exercise periods; provide a toy in his stable or field.

Whilst some steps can be taken, such as removing the horse's droppings as soon as they are passed, it is essential that the root cause of the coprophagia is attacked. Simply muzzling the horse so he cannot eat droppings, or tying him up, will only create other frustrations and habits. If your measures do not succeed, then consult your vet.

Jumping out of Fields

Horses and ponies which jump out generally do so for a reason, and an animal kept alone will have every excuse to go walkabout: horses are gregarious creatures and are meant to live in groups. Another horse being ridden past could provide just the incentive the one on its own needs to tackle its field fence. If you do have a lone horse then provide some company in the form of sheep or cattle – or offer a home to a companion pony, for example from an equine welfare/rescue centre. Many of the animals at these centres are not suitable for ridden work but would be fine as a companion.

Ensure that your fencing and gates are high enough and strong enough to prevent horses either jumping over or breaking through. Make sure that the lower part of any hedging is reinforced with timber as some ponies are expert at getting on their knees and squeezing or wiggling through gaps.

Electric fencing, used inside your field fencing, may deter escapees, provided that the horse has been introduced to electric fencing and knows that a shock will result if he gets too close. If your horse does live alone, tethering is a possibility but you must ensure that he has access to water, can shelter from the elements if needed, and is not vulnerable to attacks from unscrupulous and mindless vandals. Children can also victimise tethered ponies: it is not unknown for ponies to have been stoned as part of a children's game. Tethering is not feasible if other animals are loose in the field as they could become tangled up in the tethered animal's rope. You must move the tethering place regularly so that the horse has access to sufficient grazing.

Some people feel that keeping the horse stabled the whole time is the only option: this is extremely unfortunate, as horses are intended to have their liberty and often need it in order to say 'on course' temperamentally. In this case, consider yarding him. Naturally you will need to ensure the yard perimeter fence is strong and high; many livery places are converted from farmyards which often have walled areas, and with a bit of imagination these can be made into suitable crew yards.

SUMMARY

- Always consider how your horse's domesticated lifestyle conflicts with his instinctive needs.

- Ensure you apply good horse management principles at all times to reduce the likelihood of problems arising: for example, horses like a routine with the same feeding times; allow plenty of time each day for the horse to be out at grass; and so on.

- Bear in mind the pecking order of the horses in your yard so that you can avoid unnecessary distress both when they are out at grass or when stabled.

- If one horse is being bullied take action before a nasty injury occurs.

- Always try to get to the root cause of the problem rather than just treating the symptoms.

- Allow yourself plenty of time when dealing with a problem.

- Learn to control your temper; if you let aggression get the better of you, the end result will be more problems, particularly if your horse if the sensitive type.

- Rough handling will produce horses with problems which will manifest themselves in various ways.

- Some problems – for example, weaving – need to be declared when a horse is sold, and the price should reflect this. If you are in the position of buying, you may be able to find a horse which suits your needs and which is cheaper because it has a 'hang-up'; if you can cope with this, you may have a real bargain.

The wary horse will try to have a really good look at anything he feels is unfamiliar

A typical reaction to a 'monster': head and tail raised, body tense, and snorting

RIDDEN PROBLEMS

Before a horse can respect you when you are in the saddle
he has to respect you on the ground.
It is important that he does so, too, but this stage can only be reached
if he does not fear you and if he sees you as his leader.
Moreover just as you have to earn respect from the people
you work with, so you have to earn the respect of a horse.
Understanding how he sees the world, and how he reacts to it,
will assist you in reaching this goal.

Horses

are our best teachers: we can learn from them, as much as they learn from us. One of the best known adages in the horse world is 'don't put two novices together' – so don't buy a green youngster if you know nothing, because neither of you will know anything! The best buy for an inexperienced rider is a schoolmaster horse or pony; and learning from an experienced horse is the best way to become a better teacher for your next one.

Even if you have your own horse it is worth having lessons on others as often as you can afford. Each one throws up its own difficulties, and it is only by learning how to ride each individual well, so as to bring out the best of its ability, that your own riding will progress. Furthermore, lessons are invaluable for preventing those bad habits creeping in, and for improving your seat and the application of the aids. When mounted you need an independent seat, a focussed mind and control of the horse's hindquarters in order to maintain his respect.

Relaxed, happy, forward-going and responding to the lightest of aids: this young horse was sent to Max in order to give it a good start in life

Horse Slow to Answer the Leg Aids

A rider's objective is for the horse to respond to the lightest of aids. A young horse in the early stages of education ought to react to the voice, so make use of this: thus at the same time as you ask him with your leg aids to walk on, use your voice as well. As he gets the idea, then you can stop using the voice.

If the horse does not respond to your leg aid at first, then re-apply the leg but with a little more pressure. If there is still no response, then reinforce the leg aid with the use of your schooling whip. Adopt this approach right from the start, and a horse generally learns to respond well to the leg. There is no point in just applying stronger leg pressure if the horse does not move forwards. A tap with the whip will sharpen up his ideas and you will avoid the risk of him becoming so used to strong leg pressure that he just ignores it altogether.

REASONS

A horse may be slow to respond to your leg aids for various reasons:

- A young horse may be unsure about what you want.
- The horse may have been 'desensitised' to the leg aids: that is, a rider has constantly hammered his sides with his or her legs instead of lightening the aid when he responded, and as a result he has 'switched off' to the aids (this is also known as being dead to the leg).
- The rider may be telling the horse to go forwards with his legs, but he could be pulling back with the hands at the same time so the horse is receiving contradictory signals.
- If the horse is normally responsive but does not comply with your aids in particular circumstances, it could be because he is afraid or wary of what you are asking him to do; for example, he may be reluctant to go into water.
- A normally responsive horse may be trying to tell you that he is uncomfortable or in pain by refusing to go forwards with his usual *joie de vivre*.

The water is not particularly welcoming as far as this horse is concerned, but he is not objecting violently and with positive encouragement from his 'leader' – that is, his rider – he soon overcame his anxiety

However, when a horse is unsure about what you are asking him to do – such as go into water – do give him the chance to explore and test the going. Enlist the help of another horse and rider to give you a lead; once a young horse realises there is no danger, he will usually go quite cheerfully past what he might have thought was a monster. Remember that you, as the leader in the partnership, should give him confidence – and he should follow you, if you show by example that where you are asking him to go is safe.

If your horse has had a problem in the past due to pain or discomfort, but this has been sorted out, you then have to take him back to basic acceptance of the leg and hand. Once you have started this process, you must try not to push him: allow him to make mistakes, let him stop, even – and then make the situation intolerable for him. Max achieves the latter by using a soft rope (see p99) which he slaps against the horse's sides, effectively blocking off his avenues of escape and making the situation uncomfortable for him. When he steps forwards the rider must cease using the rope. If the horse stops again, however, then the rope is brought into action again. This method can be used in all kinds of situations: if the horse is reluctant to go into water, if he roots himself to the ground, if he decides he is not going to go into an indoor school, and so on.

A crucial aspect of any remedial action is its timing: notice that when a horse decides it is not going anywhere it raises its head six or eight inches or so; this is because it must displace its weight onto its hindquarters in order to gain control of the situation. This is the horse's warning sign that something is going to go wrong, and it happens just before he gives up and stops. Once you know this and can recognise it as such, then you can apply the rope as a schooling measure – if you can successfully interrupt a horse's motivating thought pattern you can school him away from an habitual way of behaving.

You must anticipate, think as the horse thinks, and try to resolve the situation *before* his thought becomes a physical action. It is generally the older horses which are more dominant and try to take control, and these are used to seeing the hand coming up and feeling the sting of the whip, up and down on one side. By using the soft rope which goes up and over the other side, the horse is baffled: you are making life uncomfortable for him, rather than causing a sting. The second he takes a step forwards you must stop the rope action and praise him. If he does not go forwards, then apply the rope again immediately.

Horse in Front of the Leg
A rider wants his horse to be in front of the leg in as much as when he asks it to do something it responds immediately, without argument. However, some horses are so quick off the mark that it can be a worrying experience.

If a horse tends to rush off the instant it feels your leg, you will need to take the time to establish why this is happening. Horses will often run away from pain, and this can take many forms; it may be the physical pain of a trapped nerve or a badly fitting saddle, or possibly the memory of a rough rider who constantly yanked him in the mouth.

Once the cause of pain has been identified and resolved you will probably find that the horse still has a tendency to rush off, particularly if the pain-related problem has been with him for some time, and it will probably be quite a while before he realises that the pain is no longer there. You can help him by working him on circles in an enclosed arena, using your weight aids to slow him down rather than pulling on his mouth – as soon as you pull, he pulls back, and so on, a vicious circle. Practise with halt and walk transitions initially. He has probably been rushing along on his forehand, so slowing down will encourage him to bring his hindquarters more underneath his body and to start to take more weight on them and less on the forehand.

It may take time for him to answer the aids without zooming off, but praise him when he does. Start to use trot as well, just trotting for a few strides before returning to walk. Vary the number of strides for which you trot and walk so that he doesn't start to anticipate.

A common solution with a horse that is onward bound is to change to a stronger bit. This often compounds the problem, however, and does

Before you can start to deal with a horse's problems you have to be sure that your own riding is not causing the difficulties, so it is vital that you have regular lessons from a knowledgeable person; it is all too easy to fall into bad habits. Remember that the horse's way of going reflects how he is being ridden, so instead of blaming your horse for any difficulties, first consider that it may be *you* that are causing them. Subtle changes in your position may be having an effect on him – and it is obvious that the more serious the faults in your riding, the more dramatic may be the effect on the way the horse goes.

not address the root cause; if the horse is sharp because of, say, tooth problems, a more severe bit will very often aggravate the situation. Changing to a less severe bit may help – but only once the real cause of the problem has been addressed.

An aversion to the rider's leg is often found in a horse that is a nervous type itself, so more preparation is needed before a rider gets on. A great deal of handling around the horse's sides is needed in order to desensitise it; work on its vulnerable areas, in particular around the girth and the stifle, using lots of gentle patting. Although the horse will flinch the minute you pat him, keep patting softly and in this way you train him not to react violently against touch. Lungeing on two lines also helps because the lines touch the horse's sides where the rider's legs will be applied. The more the horse becomes accustomed to feeling something in these areas, the better it is for him.

Running Backwards

A backward-thinking horse can become extremely efficient at travelling in reverse in order to avoid doing as his rider asks. In effect, running back is a serious version of napping and the potential for accident is high. Such horses must be taught to go forwards from the leg – although first you have the immediate problem of how to cope with the reversing. If strong use of legs, spurs and whip has no effect, you may be able to break his backward momentum by turning him to one side or the other. If it is feasible, let him back himself into a prickly hedge or something solid; this will usually quite effectively send him forwards – though try to avoid going backwards into a ditch as the potential for injury is high. Should the horse behave in this way at home, you could arrange for a nimble-footed assistant to be on hand, who may be able to send the horse forwards using a lunge whip or a stable broom.

The 'soft rope', which has a number of uses: for a horse that is dead to the leg; to attract the attention of a horse that is prone to shying; for an animal which refuses to move. The idea is that by using the rope on alternate sides, the situation is made uncomfortable for the horse as his avenues of escape are blocked. His alternative is to step forwards. When he does this he is rewarded by the rider ceasing to use the rope

Send the horse forwards strongly as soon as you have managed to stop him running back. Alternatively some people have found that a good way of stamping out the habit is to make him go on going backwards even when he wants to stop.

If, however, the horse is napping through fear then you have to approach the problem differently, for imposing more nasty experiences will only reinforce his conviction that he should have escaped in any way possible. A sensible approach with a young horse is to allow him to stretch his head down and look at the object which is worrying him; also to have an older horse to escort him past it.

There are different schools of thought regarding the value of teaching a horse to rein back. Some people feel that it should not be taught to rein back until the idea of going forwards on the aids is thoroughly established in its mind. On the other hand, some people feel that teaching it to rein back should be an early part of its training so that the rider can use this to his advantage. For example, if a horse refuses to pass a particular object and spins round, some people advocate reining back past the object and only then turning the horse and progressing as normal. Others maintain that if a horse starts to run backwards, as long as it has been taught to rein back, the rider can effectively take control and insist that it continues to go backwards until *he* allows it to stop.

Allowing a horse to explore new 'territory' – for example water or lorries – in his own time will pay dividends; when he has made his mind up that there is nothing to worry about, he will just get on with life

Shying

In a wild state the horse must be wary of any strange object simply because its prime concern is to survive. And in spite of thousands of years of domestication, horses still retain this basic instinct and live by it. Thus if something changes in their normal environment – for instance, if roadworks are started along a normal hacking route, or a bag of rubbish is dumped in the hedgerow of their field – then they have to establish whether or not this intrusion is a source of danger. Partly through fear and partly through curiosity they will use their senses of sight and smell to establish what's what. Moreover it is not simply a case

of one glance at the object and one sniff: horses will sniff and touch things repeatedly in order to satisfy themselves. Just watch any group of young horses exploring the world: some will be bolder than others, but they will all examine any new object thoroughly. As long as you allow a youngster to do this, he will then be able to satisfy himself that the wheelbarrow or the muck skip, or whatever it is, is not going to attack him, and he will therefore no longer show any fear.

The other important point to appreciate regarding shying is that horses see the world differently from us, and so may react strongly to things that we barely see. They can detect very slight movements: circus horses, for instance, will respond to extremely subtle instructions from their trainers, signals which the audience may not even notice; and sometimes a horse will shy violently at something imperceptible, catching the rider quite by surprise – if you can see a hazard ahead you will be ready should your horse misbehave, but if the object causing him to shy is invisible, then you may soon be in trouble!

Horses do have a wider field of vision than humans, and as they are used to seeing a number of things at any one time it can be more difficult for them to focus on any one object – and if that object is on the ground then the horse will have to shift his position in order to see it properly. Depending on where it is situated he may have to lower his head, tilt it to one side, or even move his whole body to one side – in other words, shy. Whether or not he is moving also influences how he sees things; in fact it is far more difficult for him to focus on the move, which is why he will generally try and stop in order to look at things.

You may have to contrive to set up some situations so that your horse can become used to certain 'monsters'. Allow yourself plenty of time, but never imagine that you can beat your horse into accepting something which frightens him; if you beat him you will only succeed in reinforcing his anxieties

When the horse's head is straight he can see what is in front of him, or he can see to the side and the rear – but he cannot do both at the same time. How many times have you experienced a horse shying at something in front of him, and then unexpectedly shooting forwards because something has come up behind him and frightened him?

It really is vital for riders to understand just why a horse reacts as he does – that shying is a reflex action and is therefore impossible to 'beat' out of him. In essence, when a horse shies away from something, he is simply putting a 'flight' distance between him and the object; once he is what he considers to be a 'safe' distance from the hazard he can take stock of the situation and decide what to do next.

Many horses have a wide range of tricks which they will quite happily use against their rider

What can be done is to train the horse so that instead of automatically reacting to his instinct he looks to his rider for leadership and safety. If he is ridden by someone who is ineffective or worried, then the fact that he is not being given clear leadership signals will reinforce his view that the object is potentially dangerous and should be avoided.

When dealing with shying you must therefore be positive and confident; if you are not, then you will create more problems for yourself. Keep alert when hacking out, riding your horse 'on the aids' so that you are prepared for anything. If he is sufficiently well schooled then use leg-yielding or shoulder-in to manoeuvre him past an object which frightens him; turning his head away from it means that he will see it in a less distorted way. Using the soft rope (refer to the section on the horse being behind the leg) is also useful. If the horse is peering into the hedgerow or staring at something on the verge, you want him to concentrate on *you*: tapping him on the offside with the rope will divert his attention to that side and you can then apply your offside leg and hand and leg-yield into the verge and past the offending object. Leg-yield is used because you want the horse to get closer to the object rather than further away from it. If you can control the horse and persuade him to face up to his worries about things, then the next time something makes him anxious his instinct to move away will not be so urgent – basically you are interrupting what can be a vicious circle. Once horses have concentrated their attention onto something, you will find it very difficult to pull their heads round; hence the need to divert their attention. However, remember that the rope is complementary to your aids and cannot work in isolation. Hack out a youngster in the company of an older, more sensible and worldly-wise horse; the older horse can then give it a lead, even standing by the object whilst the youngster is allowed to stop, touch and sniff it.

With the roads nowadays being so busy it is a sensible idea to set up scenarios at home before you even venture out on your horse. Under safe conditions at home you can introduce him to cones, signs, tractors, cars, bikes, prams and all kinds of potential hazards so that when he meets the real thing out on the roads he will be confident and unconcerned about them. The police prepare their horses in this way. If you do not allow your horse to confront his fears, then you are in effect giving him the chance to become more nappy. It is just like us humans and our fears: we can *teach* ourselves to tolerate things we dislike, such as spiders, flying and snakes.

Of course, there are some horses which delight in fooling their riders, pretending that 'monsters' are lurking everywhere; these need to be ridden forwards strongly. It would also be sensible to review your horse's feed and exercise programme, particularly if overfreshness is causing him to shy.

Napping

A horse may become nappy for several reasons: it may purely and simply be evading the rider's aids because it wants to stay with its companions; it may have lost confidence or may feel insecure; it may

There are many reasons why a horse becomes nappy, and it is the rider's responsibility to establish why: is he bored or tired, or thoroughly sick of competitions? Is he being stubborn because something is hurting? It is important to look past the symptoms and to work out what is happening in the horse's mind, and why: only then can you find a meaningful solution

YOUR HORSE'S FUTURE IS IN YOUR HANDS...

Even if your main interest is only hacking, do not neglect your horse's general schooling. If ever you need to sell him, he will be much more attractive to prospective purchasers if he is supple, obedient and reasonably schooled; and if he can meet his owner's needs, then he is less likely to be sold on. It is much more difficult to find good homes for horses which apparently have no particular talents or are ill-mannered and poorly schooled.

be nappy through stubbornness or bad temper; or because it is bored or tired. In short, it is your responsibility to establish the cause, and to try to remedy it. For example, if you always take the horse on the same hack, always turning round at the same point, this is soul-destroying for both horse and rider. Therefore organise his work programme so that it includes hacking out alone and with other horses, schooling sessions, jumping, going to competitions or to sponsored rides, riding out to different areas – in short, plenty of variety to keep his mind fully occupied as well as his body.

Even if you intend to do no more than hack around the countryside, it is important to include regular schooling in his exercise programme, for this will ensure that he stays supple and obedient to your aids, and is generally a more pleasurable ride. If he is better schooled, this in itself is bound to improve the quality of your hacks; for instance, if he will perform a turn on the forehand, opening and shutting gates will be very much more easily accomplished; and shoulder-in can be most usefully employed to get a horse past something which frightens him with a minimum of fuss.

There is no doubt that some horses are stubborn and bad -empered – but if yours is like this, are you sure there isn't an underlying cause for this attitude or temperament? For example, he may be bad tempered because he is in pain. Similarly, some horses can only communicate the fact that something hurts by being stubborn. The most difficult part of sorting out any problem is realising what the true cause is: seeing past the symptoms, realising that they are only symptoms, and appreciating that you have to dig deeper and use your head to work out what is really happening and why.

The animal's instinctive behaviour has to be considered, too: horses are gregarious and like to be with their own kind, so not unnaturally they are reluctant to leave other horses. In the wild when danger is evident, horses bunch together for protection, and domestic horses will also do this when they are out in their fields. It follows, therefore, that to hit a frightened horse to get him away from what he considers to be the safety of his companions does not make much sense. Horse sales are a case in point, where worried, insecure, frightened horses can be seen bunching together. When an individual horse has to be sent into the ring or into a lorry it will, quite naturally, nap; and although it is not supposed to happen, horses are hit with sticks to get them to move forwards.

A horse lacking in confidence should be taken back to the manège and worked through basic schooling exercises to get him thinking forwards and responding to your voice (for example, when lungeing and long-reining), and then reacting to your aids when being ridden. Perhaps the loss of confidence has resulted from an accident whilst out hacking, in which case once schooling has re-established a measure of self-assurance, the horse should be hacked out in the company of other confident horses and riders. Being alert is vital when riding: thus when you feel the horse hesitate you can send him on with your aids, reinforced by your stick and voice if necessary. Positioning your body slightly behind the vertical makes this task easier.

If your horse does stop and refuses to go forwards, try circling tightly, using a great deal of inside leg to generate movement. After a few circles send him on again. You may need to repeat this several times for him to get the idea that you are not going to accept his evasions.

Running Away and Pulling

When a horse truly bolts he is in a blind panic and unaware of what the rider is telling him, though fortunately this does not happen very often. Many horses take charge and go faster than the rider wants them to, but this is not bolting.

Being run away with is not a pleasant experience, however. It may develop from the horse pulling and becoming progressively stronger. Often the first reaction when a horse starts to get strong is to put a stronger bit in its mouth. However, more important is to determine why the horse is pulling. In many cases there is some discomfort or pain, for example from teeth which have not been rasped, from ill-fitting tack (saddle and bridle) or from a rider who is bouncing heavily on the horse's back. If your horse has a drop noseband, check its fitting: if it is too low it will be restricting his breathing which may cause him to panic.

Get your horse's teeth, back and tack checked. Is there a conformational problem which has a bearing on the horse's behaviour? Once these have been examined and eliminated, go back to re-schooling. Try using a milder bit, such as a thick German snaffle or rubber snaffle fitted slightly higher in the mouth; this is an effective solution with many horses. A hackamore is another alternative. Each horse is an individual and must be treated as such.

The horse must also learn to respect the rider's leg, and although it may seem illogical when you are going faster than you like, it is important to have the legs on the horse's sides at all times. If you always ride with your legs away from his sides, then he will never learn either to accept or to respect the leg aids.

When riding an onward-bound horse or a puller, a rider tends not to use his legs. You can see here how the rider's lower legs are not at all in contact with the horse's sides. However, it is vital that a horse does accept the leg aids, and that a rider uses the aids correctly. Your horse should react to you, not the other way round

The main problem with re-schooling a puller is that it will inevitably take months of patient work to put right the incorrect muscle development and way of going. Horses which pull have certain physical characteristics which are a clear indication as to the way they behave – for instance, the muscle on the underside of their neck is always extremely well developed as they are generally used to going round on their forehand with their heads in the air; they therefore lack the curve of muscle on the top of their neck found in horses which accept the rider's contact and move forwards with the impulsion generated from behind. Also their hocks and quarters tend to trail out behind them instead of being more underneath their body, ready to provide the impulsive energy.

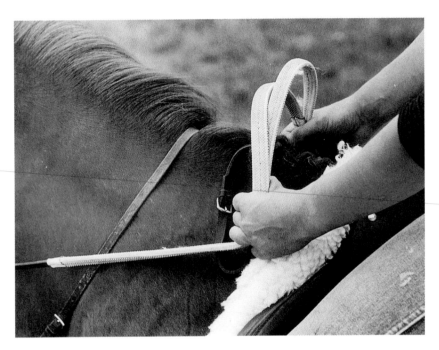

When a horse is so much accustomed to this way of going he will find it difficult to slow down and work in a more efficient outline with his quarters underneath him and accepting the rider's contact. However, as long as the puller's problem can be sorted out – by resolving any pain or discomfort, if this is what is making him misbehave – then the horse will be in a better frame of mind to start re-learning.

Bridging the reins, as shown, is often advised if riding a hard-pulling horse. However, if you are in a safe environment it sometimes works to throw the reins at the horse so he has nothing to pull against, and keep him going even when he wants to stop. After a few sessions he will realise that pulling does not mean he gets his own way

There is a new training aid called the 'Harbridge' (also available in the USA) which does help with the re-schooling of pullers; it is an elasticated device which provides resistance if the horse puts his head in the air, but which when fitted properly will slacken as soon as he submits to the rider's hand – and horses soon realise that it is more comfortable to lower their heads and necks. It is only to be used on the flat.

If you find yourself being run off with, what can you do? Exerting a continuous pull on the reins is useless as your horse is inevitably much stronger than you are. Taking a pull, then releasing, then taking a pull and releasing again and so on works in steadying some horses. If you have room, try to circle the horse and keep spiralling inwards until the circle is much smaller and you can regain control. Turn the horse's head to the left, because most horses naturally find the left side easier. When a horse pulls he generally has his head in the air, so try to get the head down – but don't haul backwards or you will raise the head even more. Keep your hands low and try to spiral in.

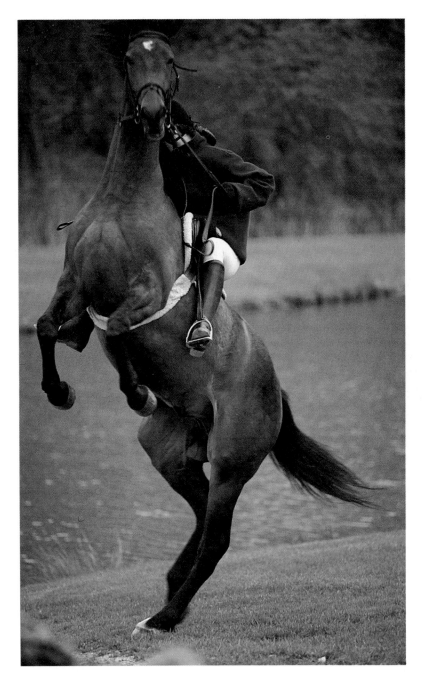

Rearing is a problem feared by many riders – the idea of the horse losing its balance and coming over on to the rider is particularly worrying. You can see here how the horse's underside is exposed and it is this, plus the fact that a horse goes into pressure, that Max uses as part of his solution for rearers

Rearing

Without any doubt at all, rearing is one of the most disconcerting of the horse's possible disobediences, and one which can easily result in injury to both rider and horse. If a horse rears, the rider *must* go forwards – hanging on to the reins could result in the horse being pulled off balance and falling backwards on to you. Moreover, as you go forwards, go to one side slightly or you are likely to receive a clout from the horse's neck in your face, which can be rather painful. Also if you do this you can grab hold of the horse's neck with your arm to steady yourself if necessary – and with your other hand you might try

An inexperienced rider should not attempt to deal with a rearing horse. Rearing is potentially a very dangerous habit, and the risk of injury is greater when the rider is unable to balance properly without the aid of the reins.

Bucking can also be a big problem for the more novice rider – if a horse is serious about putting you on the floor, there is little chance of an everyday rider staying on. And with injuries a very real possibility, the least the inexperienced rider will get away with is a total loss of confidence. Such an occurrence may well be devastating for you – so don't risk physical or emotional injuries by trying to deal with a horse which is too much for you.

to pull the horse's neck sideways, because he will then have to put his front feet down (the head and neck are his balancing pole, and he can't rear if his neck is pulled round to one side).

It is very often the case that serious rearing developed from something which was no more than a cheeky little evasion to start with, but which, left uncorrected, grew into a full-blown habit and problem. Traditional remedies for curing a rearer included such bizarre tricks as cracking an egg or a water-filled bag on the top of its head, the theory being that the trickling sensation would make it think twice about 'injuring' itself. However, horses very often seem oblivious to self-injury, for instance they will often sustain cuts without apparently noticing; yet if a human received a similar injury it is likely there would be considerable complaint and attention-seeking.

The other problem with regard to cracking something on a horse's head is that he is an interpressure animal, meaning that he moves *into* pressure rather than away from it; so that hitting a horse on the head is likely to encourage him to rear even more. Conversely, therefore, if you want to get the horse back on the ground, and knowing that he goes into pressure, then it makes sense to provide some 'contra-irritant' underneath his belly; Richard Maxwell uses a soft rope which he will slap across a rearer's exposed underbelly. However, he does not use this in isolation: by the time he reaches the stage of being able to employ such a corrective measure, Max will already have built up a relationship with the animal, and will understand its individual psychological make-up. As he is extremely experienced in dealing with problem horses and has a truly secure and independent seat, Max makes dealing with rearers look easy: it is not a remedy which should be attempted by the average rider, however.

What Max does with a rearer is to deliver a sharp smack across its belly; it reacts immediately to the pressure and comes straight down. It may, of course, rear again, when another smack is handed out – and it soon comes to realise that rearing and exposing its belly is not sensible. Moreover, this method involves only a few smacks, instead of numerous whacks from the whip as recommended in other methods of dealing with a rearer (keep it going forwards, use your whip and spurs to keep it moving, don't let it stop and rear, and so on).

In effect the horse cannot work out where the smacks are coming from: he does not associate them with his friend Max, who has taken the trouble, in the days leading up to his being ridden, to make friends with him; all he knows is that when he rears he is attacked from underneath. Instinct tells him this is dangerous, and so he decides not to expose himself to danger any more: the end result is that he no longer rears. Self-preservation is a strong motivator!

Sorting out the problem does not stop here, however; a sensible step is to reiterate basic schooling, and to re-establish that the horse goes forwards from the rider's aids as soon as he is asked.

Bucking

Bucking falls into two camps: the serious 'I really intend to get you off' kind, and the 'Hey, this is fun!' type. There are various degrees of the first sort and the main problem is learning to distinguish these, as well as recognising whether the horse is bucking because he feels playful, or because he is worried by something more serious such as pain.

Playful bucks may happen, for example, when the horse which thoroughly enjoys hunting first moves off from the meet. Whilst it would be a pity to curtail his *joie de vivre*, you have to be careful not to allow it to develop into a more troublesome habit. Insufficient work and/or time at liberty can also cause the horse to produce a few playful bucks – after all, the impulse to move around and express himself freely in a physical way is part of every horse's natural make-up, and if denied this opportunity, say, by being turned out, many resort to making their feelings known when under saddle. Just take note of how horses behave when you do turn them out for a spell of liberty in the field, especially if it is winter: many will fly off, buck, leap in the air, spin round and generally have a play, and that is a part of their nature. We should not want to extinguish their natural behaviour, but we do need to channel it.

More serious bucking which is clearly intended to deposit the rider nearly always has an underlying reason: whilst occasionally there are

Many horses and ponies buck through high spirits, but if this is allowed too frequently it may get out of hand and become a habit. Bucking can also be a way in which the horse tries to communicate to the rider that it is suffering pain or discomfort

rogue horses, most behavioural problems can be traced back to pain or discomfort. This may be caused by a badly fitting saddle, a dirty numnah which is rubbing, a pinching girth, or pain in the horse's back or another part of his body – though some horses do take advantage of the fact that they can get rid of their rider through bucking and therefore avoid work. These will need an experienced rider to teach them that their technique is not always effective and that they may as well get used to working again.

Basically, bucking is a way of resisting the forward driving aids, so if you can keep the horse moving forwards strongly it will not be able to buck. It is also important to keep the horse's head up because once he gets it between his legs he can have a fine old time impersonating a rodeo horse. If a horse is starting to think about having a buck you can usually feel him hesitate so then you need to drive him forwards immediately with your seat, legs and voice reinforced by a slap from the stick if necessary. Be careful not to throw your reins away, however, because your horse will then be able to get his head down! Hold on to the saddle pommel or the mane if necessary and lean your upper body back slightly; if you adopt a forward seat you will soon be sent 'out of the front door'. In canter it is often easier to sit the bucks if you adopt a jumping seat, although you need to have a stable lower leg position.

Going along in this manner, head in the air, jogging and generally being resistant, provides an uncomfortable ride and is probably due to the horse suffering some kind of discomfort

Jogging

Jogging is an exhausting habit for both horse and rider. The rider is constantly shaken about and his patience often tested to the limits, whilst the horse wastes energy and places undue strain on his joints and tendons.

First it is important to determine why the horse jogs: thus it may be badly fitting tack; a rider's restrictive contact; rough, insensitive riding; or too much food and insufficient work or time turned out at liberty for the horse. Or perhaps the rider is gripping up and the horse is reacting to the tension, or it may be the horse's temperament; or the horse evading the rider's aids and being out of balance; or pain from teeth, neck or back problems.

Often it is not easy for a rider to admit that he or she is at fault; however, it is better to admit your problems to yourself and to correct them, than to carry on, letting the whole world see that you are at fault because of the way your horse goes! Consult with an experienced instructor if you are unsure where your riding might be improved.

Coping with the problem will take time: frustrating as it is, there is no point in yanking at the reins or pulling back. Furthermore, make sure that you sit in the saddle, and that you use your weight aids and keep your leg on – no matter how fast you are going, you still need to use your legs. If the problem is pain-related it will take some time before the horse realises that the pain has gone and breaks his habitual pattern of jogging.

Working the horse on the lunge, or long-reining him and insisting that he walks, helps to instil obedience to the voice and will prove to him that the cause of his discomfort has been removed. Under saddle you have to insist on a walk or a proper trot; thus as rider you must be consistent each day, never accepting a jog. Riding out with a steady companion often has a calming influence.

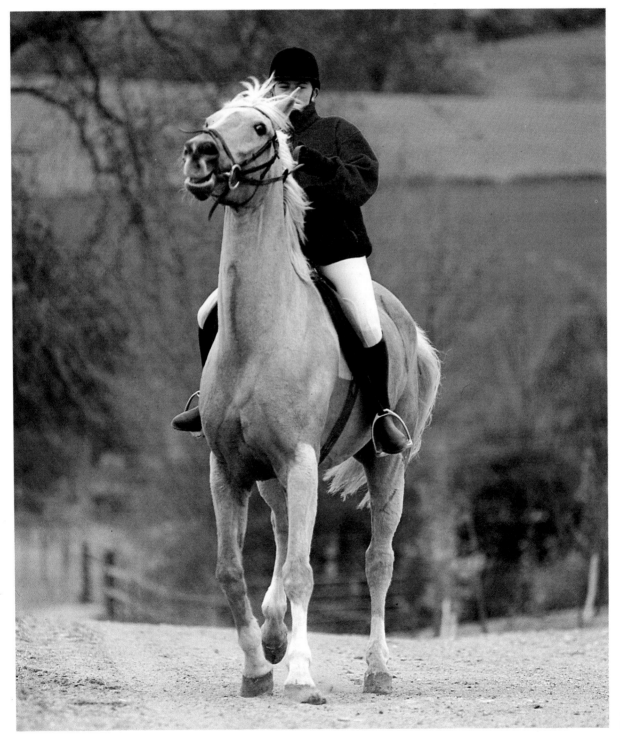

If you are in the position of being a fairly inexperienced owner with a young horse, *do* seek sensible, practical help. You may be lucky and have a youngster which is thoroughly laid back about everything; but if he is a livewire, you could soon find yourself in deep trouble. Ask around your area and find out who has a 'healthy' attitude to coping with youngsters; watch them working, follow up horses they have dealt with, ask as many of their clients as possible for their views. If someone has a good reputation you will find out – but if people are unwilling to comment on someone, or you cannot find a satisfied customer, then you should be cautious.

It is sometimes possible to prevent the habit developing by considering your hacking companions carefully, because some horses start to jog in order to keep up with other animals which have a better walk. Being asked to walk faster than is comfortable for them, or being asked to trot too slowly can lead to some horses jogging.

Refusing to Stand whilst being Mounted

There are several reasons why horses may behave in this way: poor training – they have not been taught to stand still until asked to move; they have no respect for the rider; because of pain or discomfort. When a horse moves off as it is being mounted, it is effectively running away from the rider; and if this is due to lack of respect, there are quite likely to be problems at faster paces, too, as the horse's opinion of its rider will not change when it goes into trot, canter or gallop. However, the 'running away' could also be due to pain and this avenue needs exploring before any other action is taken. If pain or discomfort is the cause, then once these have been eliminated, the horse will need re-training. The procedure for re-training is the same, whatever the reason for his behaviour, whether it is lack of respect, or poor education, or pain.

You will need three assistants, as well as plenty of patience and a calm attitude. Consider your method of mounting the horse: if at all possible use a mounting block as this minimises strain on the horse's back, is less effort for you, and is less likely to cause damage to the saddle. Whilst we all need to be supple enough to be able to mount from the floor, there is no shame in using a mounting block and it is really far more sensible to do so, from all points of view.

You will need someone to hold the horse whilst you mount. If his behaviour when being mounted is excessive – for example, if he takes off at a great rate – then if possible conduct your lessons in an enclosed area such as an indoor school, and have an assistant on each side to help hold him. Beware of standing directly in front of him if he has a tendency to rush forwards. Ensure that your handlers are equipped with 'safety' wear, namely hats, gloves and protective boots.

To begin with it is essential to use a mounting block so that you can mount and sit down gently in the saddle; for the horse to have a rider slumping down on his back with no consideration at all for his welfare is a sure way of abusing his tolerance, and asking for him to walk off. Reward him if he does stand still with a pat and your voice, then ride him forwards. Practise this several times. If you do not have a helper you can position the horse against a wall.

Those responsible for educating a young horse can considerably influence its future attitude to being mounted in the way they initially approach this aspect of starting (breaking in). Well before your young horse is introduced to the saddle you can prepare him for the experience of being tacked up and ridden. The first essential is to gain his confidence; then you can proceed by standing with one arm over his back, patting him from this position; make sure he is used to you standing alongside, raising your arms up and then placing them over his back. You could then try leaning over him. Let the youngster sniff and touch a numnah or saddle pad before you place it over his back. If this is done as part of daily life it will become 'ordinary', and the actual process of a saddle being put on will be less of a trauma.

As part of his initial training it is a good idea to stand on the youngster's nearside and quietly jump up and down; this will prepare him for a rider being legged up, and eventually mounting from the ground. By getting the horse used to this kind of activity over a period of time we are in effect 'de-sensitising' him and persuading him to be less inclined to follow his natural instincts.

Rushing at Fences

There may be several reasons why a horse rushes his fences: a lack of confidence or preparation; fear or pain; and the rider's attitude or style of riding may be the cause. Horses which have been overfaced – that is presented at jumps which are beyond their current level of ability – may react by henceforth galloping at all fences in a rather

Very few horses genuinely bolt, but being on a hard-pulling horse can be a scary experience. Don't try and pull back because the horse will always win a battle of strength

panic-stricken way, or by refusing to jump at all. Confidence can also be dented if, for instance, the horse has a nasty fall when jumping; if he is then ridden by a strong, determined rider he will have little chance of refusing or running out so will probably resort to speed. Fear plays a part here, too.

In addition the horse could be afraid of what might happen if he got the jump wrong – if at some time he had been beaten for making a mistake, then this recollection and the fear of more whipping and spurring could be a powerful influence. Horses which have been insufficiently prepared and schooled for jumping could well end up rushing; some animals find it all extremely exciting and if this enthusiasm is not handled properly early on, then the result may well be a very onward-bound horse and a serious accident at some point in the future.

If the horse is introduced to jumping by suddenly being faced with a fence, then it could well rush because it feels so anxious. In the very first stages of training it is better to make use of trotting poles, building up to small fences, and to use small grids or lines of fences to make jumping an enjoyable part of your horse's routine. Gridwork – also known as gymnastic jumping – has the added advantage of steadying a rushing horse because it is obliged to check itself in order to take a good look at the line of fences in front of it, and it has to use itself properly in order to negotiate so many jumps in succession.

Physical problems such as a bad back, sore feet or pain in the mouth could cause a horse to rush its fences. Pain caused from badly fitting tack can also have adverse effects.

The influence of the rider should be considered, too: if the horse receives a heavy jab in the mouth from an unbalanced, insensitive rider each time he jumps, then he will either 'run away' over it in order to get the task over quickly, or he will refuse to jump at all. If, in refusing to jump, he is beaten, then he may choose the least hurtful way and simply rush his fences.

Some riders do habitually ride at their fences at a great pace, chasing the horse off its stride and with legs and arms flailing like a tornado. Ridden like this for a while, any horse will become accustomed to approaching his fences in a rush, and will continue to do so with a new rider, until he is re-schooled.

Riders who are scared of the fence themselves may try to overcome their anxiety by riding at it very strongly, and the horse therefore approaches at a much faster pace than normal. In this case it is obviously the rider's fears which need to be addressed.

Refusing to Jump

Some of the points mentioned above (Rushing at Fences) apply here, too. For instance, a heavy-handed rider using a severe bit will soon discourage a horse: even the most saintly of jumpers will be thoroughly

LOOK TO YOURSELF FIRST

Having observed countless horses and riders in the course of lessons, it must be said that the vast majority of problems stem from the rider. Even with the more experienced combinations, a knowledgeable expert can pick up on a couple of small things which the rider has not realised he is doing – and once these are corrected, the horse starts to improve! So even if you think you are not to blame for your horse's difficulties, do seek a second opinion; in a matter of minutes your whole outlook on your 'problems' could be altered!

disconcerted if they are constantly hurt in the mouth. Pain may be related to a physical problem such as navicular in one or even both forefeet; or ill-fitting tack; or it may be directly rider-related: for instance, if the rider is left behind when the horse jumps, it will probably think twice about jumping again; similarly if the rider presents the horse badly at the fence, or comes in with insufficient impulsion (it is up to the rider to generate this), or takes a line of approach which makes it difficult for the horse to take off. If we repeatedly present a horse at a fence badly then we will in effect be teaching it to stop: remember that repetition trains a horse, so if we keep repeating a bad situation then it is our fault, not the horse's, if he learns incorrectly.

It is essential that a rider instils confidence in a horse: if the rider is scared of jumping, then probably he or she will tense up and even 'freeze', and will stop giving the aids on the approach to the fence, or will drop the contact completely – all of which may well result in the horse stopping, but *it is not his fault*. Riders who are by nature anxious or worried should not even attempt to teach an inexperienced horse to jump, because all the horse would learn from such a rider is to be anxious about jumping and to be extremely wary about getting to the other side of the fence!

The way a horse is introduced to jumping will affect his whole attitude towards it as an activity: carried out sensibly and progressively

Even the most experienced of horses will start putting in a stop if ridden frequently by people who are not committed to jumping

JUMPING AT SHOWS

Some riders have more problems jumping in public than they do at home… although it is the horse which is stopping, it is usually the rider's influence which makes him do so. Horses are very sensitive and will pick up on your anxieties so at home it is as well to be jumping fences which are bigger than those you will meet in your competitions. You can also make use of mental rehearsal and visualisation techniques to ensure that your competitive performance is enhanced.

Practise a warming-up routine so that you can prepare for your round, safe in the knowledge that it will give your horse the best chance of being ready to jump. Start off over a cross-pole, then an upright and finally a spread fence. Try to have a friend in attendance at shows to help with the warming-up procedure in the collecting ring.

so as to build confidence in both him and the rider, never allowing him to be overfaced or frightened, then most horses are co-operative. If a particular type of fence creates problems, such as a ditch, then the horse needs time and patience so that he can overcome his fear, for example schooling over shallow ditches with a lead from a more experienced horse, and gradually building up so that ditches come to be accepted as a normal part of life.

School over lots of low fences, introducing all kinds of filler and as many different types of fence as you can think of, in order to make your horse's introduction to jumping as comprehensive as possible.

Remember that when training a horse, or indeed when working any animal, it is important not to overdo things: if he is tired he cannot give of his best, and he is likely to become rebellious if pushed too far. Always have plenty of time – and never be tempted to keep on asking and asking. Confidence takes a long time to acquire, yet it can be lost in a matter of seconds: remember there is always another day.

Avoid letting the horse become sour: sourness is not conducive to co-operation, either, and some horses start to refuse simply because they are fed up with jumping. When your horse is going well it is tempting to go to one competition after another, but the end result could be a very soured animal; so plan your competitive work and plan your horse's holidays.

There may well be a very sensible, logical reason why a horse refuses to jump. Poor eyesight could be one; alternatively, his decision not to jump may be the result of an intelligent choice – one rider became very cross when her horse would not negotiate a log on a moorland ride, but it was fortunate that it ignored its rider's wishes for on the landing side was a bog.

Jumping from light into dark usually causes some consternation because a horse cannot adjust quickly to different light conditions; it is therefore a great compliment to the rider when a horse trusts him enough to jump into the dark (or to launch itself off a drop fence!).

Another factor which could cause a horse to refuse is the state of the ground: slippery or deep going soon undermines confidence, whilst constantly jumping on hard ground will jar the horse's legs. Occasionally some reverse psychology is required; for instance, Max once had a pony that stopped in front of fences without a valid reason (pain, discomfort, bad riding) and the tactics which were successfully applied were these: to send the pony on down to the fence but then to haul him up, so it was the *rider* who made the decision not to jump the fence. After a while the pony was obviously sick of being pulled to a halt and was keen to jump, and relieved to be allowed to do so.

Reverse psychology often works well with horses which have been through a few hands, simply because the sort of treatment they receive is totally different to what they have experienced before. It is rather like a shock treatment for them, although not in a nasty way.

SUMMARY

- Respect is a two-way commitment for both horse and rider.

- Don't just treat the symptoms of the problem: determine the real cause, and adapt a strategy to deal with the root problems.

- You and your horse can learn from each other.

- Ride as many horses as you can to improve your riding.

- If your horse does not respond to your aids don't keep nagging away at him or you'll just desensitise him altogether to your aids.

- In the partnership you are the leader, and you have to be positive and confident.

- If your horse's problem was rooted in pain you will have to go back to basic schooling once the pain/discomfort has been resolved. It may also take some time before the horse realises that the pain will no longer plague him.

- Learn to recognise the warning signs that something is going wrong.

- Tune in to your horse's thoughts.

- Remember that your horse sees the world differently from you, and that this affects his behaviour.

- Regular schooling is vital to your horse's suppleness and obedience, whatever the discipline you intend to follow.

- Make sure your horse is schooled to a sensible level well before you take him out on the road; the highway is not the place to start trying to teach your horse how to behave.

- Let your horse confront his fears, in a situation which you can control and from which he can learn.

- In a battle of strength the horse will always win.

- Use your superior intelligence to work out ways round problems.

- Patience is a virtue which you must possess and exercise!

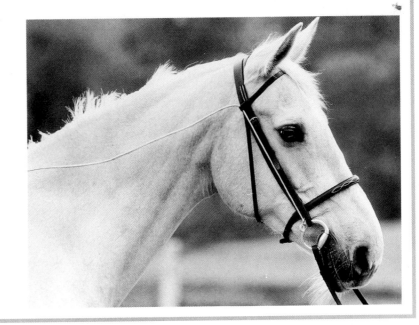

A simple, cheap way of dealing with ponies which constantly stick their heads down to eat causing their young riders to be hauled forwards is to attach baler twine as shown, securing one end to the saddle D-ring, to make a pair of 'grass reins'

CASE HISTORIES

*Hundreds of horses have passed through Max's hands,
and his belief in the methods he uses is unswerving: time and again
he has helped horses and riders enjoy a better life together.
As you will see from some of the following case histories,
a horse often has several problems and so more than one method
may be necessary to achieve the ultimate result – a happy horse.
For many horses this may mean they are pain free,
perhaps for the first time in years; and all of them
will have decided of their own free will to behave in a way
which is beneficial to both themselves and their owners.
Moreover, in every case the results are achieved without inflicting pain
on the horse, and without beating it into submission
– which in any case is never true submission.*

We hope very much that *you* can learn from the methods described, and that this way of coping with problems will help you find a solution to yours: all the following case histories can be related to everyday difficulties undoubtedly experienced by many of us. And although the methods employed to resolve them may perhaps incorporate a way of thinking new to many of us, we should all feel encouraged to try them because, as the case histories will show, they have been proved to be effective.

You never know what you may meet on a hack: on tracks such as this bridleway where the conditions are safe, give your horse the chance to confront his fear; once he has done so he is generally happy to go past it – though note how the ear and eye closest to the 'monster' is locked on to it, just as a precaution

A Solution to Flighty, Over-Excitable Behaviour

Very flighty, over-excited horses can be a danger to themselves and to others – the sort that leaps for a hundred metres if a pheasant appears from the hedge, or panics at the slightest opportunity, running off and possibly hurting itself or its rider. The procedure we call 'sacking out' can be most helpful with these: after 'sacking out' the horse is much calmer and less inclined to panic, so that its general behaviour under saddle and when handled is vastly improved. The equipment necessary for 'sacking out' is a large plastic sheet (measuring about 6 x 4ft/1.8 x 1.2m) and plenty of time, a period of days if necessary. The sheet must be folded up until it is small enough to fit into the hand; then tap and scrunch it all over the horse – its skin will flinch (as it does when a fly

The 'sacking out' procedure described here would benefit this horse as it would desensitise him to sudden sounds and movements

lands on it) but the whole point of the exercise is to keep touching it all over until it stops flinching. (This assumes that it has already joined up with you, and knows that it is better off to stay with you than to move away from you.)

The next stage is to open the sheet out a little and repeat the procedure; sometimes there is not a great deal of reaction from the horse until the sheet is opened out considerably. However, it is important not to proceed to the next stage until the horse is completely unfazed by the current one and will happily accept the sheet being tapped all over its body; make sure you go over its back and between its back legs, too. Working through three folds of the sheet will probably take 60–90 minutes. Providing the horse accepts what you have done you can then stop and return to the procedure the next day – though you may have to go back a step when you start off on the second day.

The whole procedure may take a week or longer, but ultimately you should be able to shake and flap the sheet at the horse from every direction and angle, so that it remains unperturbed and shows absolutely no panic reaction. This process is similar to the scrunching of aluminium foil which is carried out with young foals (part of the foal imprinting system mentioned earlier); what it does in effect is to desensitise the horse to sudden sound, movement and touch. 'Sacking out' is therefore one of the best ways of preparing a horse for the unexpected, particularly those worried by, for example, noisy or flapping tarpaulins on lorries or tractors, barking dogs, cyclists or motorcyclists whizzing past.

Some horses can be prepared for 'sacking out' by being made to spend a certain length of time – usually a day or two – in a 'bag box': this is a normal loosebox, but with several empty feed bags suspended from the ceiling. Horses which are headshy or nervous soon realise that the bags will not hurt them and become used to moving around the box, eating their feed, drinking and basically just living, with the bags touching them.

'Sacking out' asks the horse to tolerate a situation which his natural instincts find hard to put up with. In addition, you take the horse to the point where no matter what happens, it stays with you, instead of the flight instinct immediately taking over.

Some racehorses work brilliantly at home but their nerves cannot cope with the racecourse atmosphere and razzmatazz: sacking out helps these to keep calm and to cope with the situation. Obviously it is impossible to school horses in a racecourse situation because courses are only open on race days; and then, those horses which are highly excitable by nature and intolerant of noise and movement anyway, find that the rush of adrenalin is just too much and become all but impossible to control. The sacking-out procedure means that such racehorses can be taught to stay sensible in situations which they find extremely uncomfortable.

A horse we knew which certainly did benefit from being 'sacked out' was a three-quarter bred mare which originally started to misbehave owing to pain in her neck and because her pelvis was incorrectly aligned. Although these problems were resolved, the mare still associated the fact of working with pain, and used any excuse to spin round, nap and rear – a lorry approaching from behind, a bird flying out from the hedgerow or another horse suddenly appearing over the field fence were enough to set her off. It was thought that her neck problem was caused by her rider landing on it when the two had a dispute at a fence. This happened on two occasions within a very short time, and with the benefit of hindsight, it was possible for the rider to identify that the mare's increasing resistance began shortly after the jumping incidents.

Extremely quick weight displacement can cause problems for the horse, and may result from a seemingly innocuous event, for example if he slips a little as he comes down a lorry ramp, or loses his back legs as he corners – anything which requires him to find his balance suddenly and quickly.

Riders would be wise to remember that their horses are not indestructible and to look for the cause of any pain or discomfort rather than just playing with the symptoms.

YOU CAN NEVER START A HORSE TOO YOUNG...

- Sacking out can be used with young horses – you don't need to have a problem before you apply the solution!
- Remember that young horses have a mind which is like an open wndow: they can take in a great deal of information. So if they learn from an early age not to be scared by sudden noises or movements, then they will be much easier to deal with when they go to shows, or are ridden out in the countryside or along the road. As horses grow older, the 'windows' of their mind start to close: rather like the cynicism of adults as compared to the innocence of children. Thus you need to get all the 'good' information you can through to your horse at an early age in order to give him the best chance of a happy life.

Savage or Aggressive Horses

Many riders do not have to deal with really difficult horses, but there are nevertheless some animals around which are very tricky to handle: how do you cope with the horse that seems to be seriously attacking, coming at you with teeth bared and ears flat back, apparently with the full intention of making contact? In such a situation it is imperative to defuse the situation and to back down strongly by turning your back or looking submissive – avert your eyes, drop your head and hunch your shoulders: horses then feel compelled not to follow up their threats.

Knowing when to stand up to a horse and when to defuse the problem takes considerable experience and nerve, as well as a sound grounding in equine psychology and behaviour; but follow the basic principles of this 'advance and retreat' philosophy and you should be able to cope with even the most difficult animal too.

One particular owner we knew went to view an attractive black Arab; it seemed quite placid, so she did not give it a thorough trial or have it vetted, but simply took it home – and four or five hours later

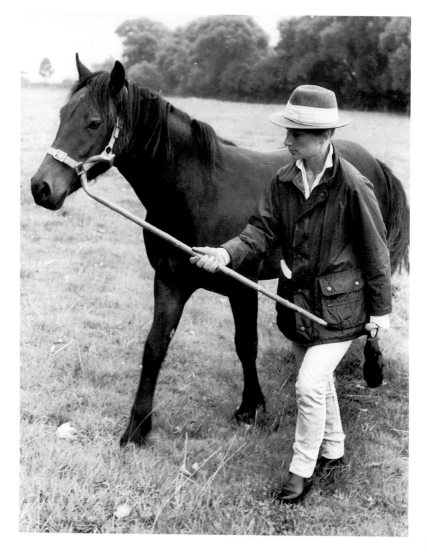

This handler carries a stick to ensure the young colt can be led without taking a chunk out of her. Just in case he tries, she has a whip as well. Although this method may have some success, it does not allow the horse the chance to enter into a partnership with his handler. Such a partnership should be based on mutual respect and the absence of fear – and it is doubtful whether this handler's method would promote those ideals

the dope which had kept it calm wore off, and it savaged its new owner. The woman needed plastic surgery. Naturally she was terrified of the horse, nor was it popular at the livery yard because when other owners went to get their horses out of the field it attacked them, too.

But crucial to this case history is the fact that the horse was terrified as well: every time anyone went into its box with stable tools it would cower in the corner, clearly indicating that at some point it had been beaten up – and those who beat up a horse don't do so in the open where everyone can see, they abuse it in its stable.

When the Arab was worked in the pen, however, it took just seven minutes for it to join up: although it was very dominant with humans, it was in fact extremely submissive to its own kind and was well down the pecking order. Because in the pen Max was communicating to the horse in its own language, it found itself confronted by its own set of rules and so became very submissive. Allowing a human into its vulnerable areas did, however, take much longer – but because every time the horse made the 'wrong' decision it was sent away to the outside perimeter of the pen and made to feel shunned, eventually it made the conscious decision to allow its belly, head, neck and legs to be handled, because this was preferable to being alienated from its new-found friend.

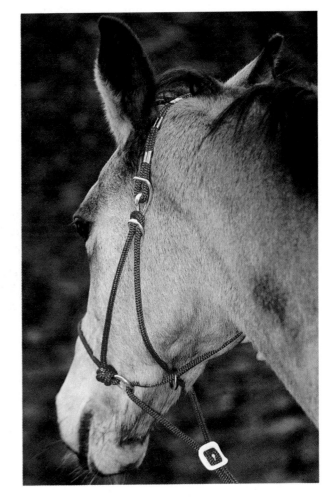

Six weeks later the horse was back with its owner, and since then the combination has been enjoying considerable success in competition; both have respect for each other and enjoy each other's company. Nevertheless, coping with such a horse takes considerable commitment on the owner's part, particularly when, as with this lady, physical injury is suffered. Someone else's brutality had produced a real problem – and the fact that its new owner lacked confidence had a negative effect on this horse.

The Be Nice halter, which exerts pressure on the poll and nose if the horse is difficult but releases as soon as the animal co-operates. Max uses a similar type of device but one which is stronger. The Be Nice is available commercially

When a horse realises he has power over people it can be an extremely tough problem to overcome; some people even feel physically sick because their horse has so much control over daily situations. Changing that scenario, and creating a partnership between human and horse where the share to the human is 51 per cent, can be a long, nerve-racking performance. Some horses are extremely strong mentally as well as physically, and many different methods must often be tried so the horse realises that committing itself to a co-operative partnership with its handler is by far the most comfortable option.

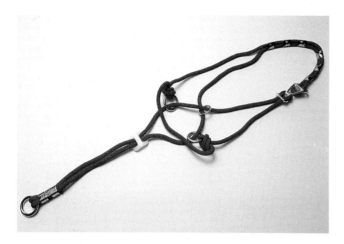

Control halters such as the Be Nice halter are not simply slapped on the horse and used with no preparation at all: the horse has to be schooled so that he understands the whole process – you cannot expect him to obey without preamble at the first jerk on the halter. If you just pull constantly on it, then you will only succeed in irritating him; the 'right' way is to put the horse in a situation where he schools himself, in the same way as the young horse is introduced to the halter

We knew another rider, a slightly built lady, who had an aggressive, bolshy horse – it was a strapping German half-bred, whose party piece was to turn its back end towards his owner and then try to squash or kick her. Although the horse 'joined up' in the pen, he was still not very amenable in the stable; it was therefore important to work with the horse in his loosebox so as to gain his respect. His owner then had to work with him, first in the pen and later in the stable, in order to establish mutual respect – but still the horse would not keep his head towards her. Max therefore showed the owner how to use a home-made device called a 'come-along' halter in order to keep control of the horse's head. (The come-along halter is similar to the Be Nice halters but more powerful; really it should only be used by people who know exactly how to use it, and are aware of its strength.)

If a horse turns its quarters to you and threatens to kick, you cannot con it into thinking you are unconcerned by screaming and flailing your arms at it. Horses know when your adrenalin is running high, and the really tough characters won't be taken in by your bravado. Persevere with the psychological approach: this is your best chance of success.

The Confirmed Rearer

Most horses are not willing seriously to challenge their human handlers psychologically; others, however, are prepared to give it a very good try, and it is difficult to come to terms with these.

It is not uncommon for stallions to rear, and if the animal is in an exciting situation then this inclination may be exhibited more frequently. Problems will arise however, if the tendency is allowed to become a habit; it can then get readily out of hand. One particular competition stallion had taken to rearing every time he entered the arena, and because he was so in control of the situation he would also walk on his hindlegs. As the problem was well established Max spent a great deal of time initially with the horse, getting to know it and building up a trusting relationship. It would have been a waste of time to have got on it and tried to sort out the rearing straightaway: many such horses tend to have experienced something which has gone wrong in their lives, and so it is necessary to go back to square one.

This particular stallion was extremely good-natured, but very cheeky – and when he realised he could get away with misbehaving, he did, taking complete control. The age-old piece of advice is to whack the horse over the head, with a whip, an egg or a breakable container filled with water. However, quite apart from being a difficult and cruel thing to do, such a measure only makes matters worse because the horse, being an 'interpressure' animal, will simply come up higher in order to meet the pressure.

Many people – even those with a great deal of experience of horses – do not appreciate this basic fact: that a horse will lean into pressure, and not away from it. Yet if you think about it, you will undoubtedly have experienced this phenomenon: for instance, when you are grooming and using firm strokes with the body brush, the horse will tend to lean into you. Another clear example of interpressure is when a horse treads on your foot and you try to push him off – the end result is that he leans more heavily onto it!

Relating this to the rearing problem, it makes sense therefore to hit the horse underneath, to encourage it to go down and into that pressure, rather than over its head. You can effectively stop a rearer like this, and without risk of any injury. Max uses a piece of soft rope with a hand loop at one end: when a horse rears, he leans down and delivers a sharp smack against its exposed belly (of course, he is very secure in the saddle). Two or three slaps is usually enough to convince even the most confirmed rearer that it is not worth exposing its vulnerable belly again. So it is effective; also it is infinitely preferable to the horse

As this horse has started to lift its feet off the floor this rider has reacted correctly in easing the rein forwards – if you use the reins to balance yourself you are in danger of pulling the horse off balance, and even over backwards

having to spend its lifetime being whipped and spurred as riders attempt to send it forwards to prevent it rearing.

Although this sounds a simple idea it is not so easy to administer, and it cannot be stressed enough that it will not work in isolation: the smacking with the rope is just one part of the whole process. It is important to appreciate that Max had already spent days with the stallion discussed here, joining up and working with it, establishing its trust and respect. When the rope treatment is applied, the horse thinks it is being attacked from the ground and does not realise that it is the rider who is administering the smack. In instinctive self-defence it stops rearing, and as no human has apparently been involved in the beating, its next reaction is to turn for reassurance to the rider it knows it can trust.

Once a horse has made this sort of voluntary decision to stop

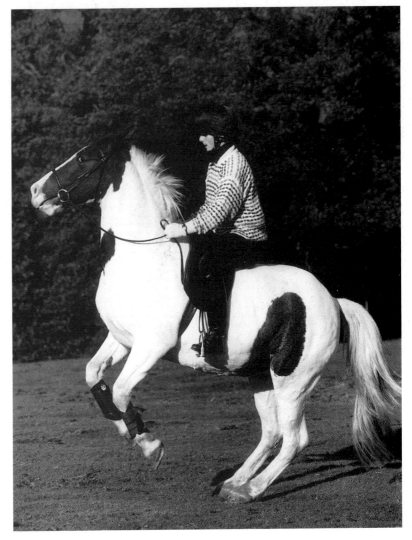

doing something, it will rarely resume its bad behaviour; insisting that it stops doing something doesn't really work, because it will not be fully committed to the new course of action – the rider must set up the situation so the horse decides for itself.

Another competition stallion we knew was very tough to overcome psychologically. It had a very dominant attitude as well as being physically strong, and all the preparatory work and the soft rope treatment failed to get through to it on a permanent basis: it was obviously going to defend its prominent position in the social hierarchy very strongly, and the problem was how to rise above it in the pecking order. In fact Max used a technique learnt in his army days to show the horse that he was the boss. The solution was simple, effective and inflicted no physical punishment – although it may not be one that the everyday rider may want to employ! He taught the horse to lie down; then whenever he felt it preparing to rear he would stop, get off, make it lie down and keep it there. As he explained: 'Making the horse lie down put him in a very vulnerable position. Even if he was out on the road I'd get off him, take him into a field and lie him down. It wore him down psychologically so that the rearing became less traumatic until eventually he stopped doing it altogether!'

Coping with the Confirmed Bucker

Horses will learn through repetition, and if this has unfortunate results for us, then it is our fault for letting such a situation develop. For example, a racehorse we had would buck furiously when its rider first mounted and continue until it threw him off; it would then behave perfectly well when the rider got on for a second time. The explanation was in fact simple: when the horse had been backed it had bucked when the saddle was first put on, and had persisted when it was mounted. The rider came off but remounted, on which occasion the horse remained calm and didn't buck. This pattern was repeated over the ensuing days – and in effect the handlers were unwittingly *schooling* the horse to buck until his rider fell off, and only behave once this objective had been achieved.

The trainers made their initial mistake in putting the rider on too soon: had they allowed the horse to 'experience' the saddle fully whilst unrestrained, then eventually it would have accepted carrying it without any initial bucking at all. In other words, they should have continued to put on just the saddle until they could do so without the horse being in the least concerned, and *only* when this point had been reached should they have thought about putting up a rider.

In this situation, repetition and retentive memory played its part in working against the human handlers. However, horses that buck generally have a problem rooted in pain – and even when this has been sorted out, the memory of the pain will still be strong and the horse may persist in bucking. There is no point in hitting it for bucking

If your horse starts to buck, consider the possible reasons; it may be more than him simply feeling full of himself

because in doing so you merely add to the pain association. No, alternative methods have to be applied.

Max has invented a device called the gumline which can be employed when dealing with such an animal: this is a piece of soft rope which slips under the horse's top lip and is then taken up alongside the bridle cheekpieces to the poll. Here it is knotted so that it is held in place against the top lip, though without causing any discomfort. It then follows the crest of the neck to the saddle where it is attached. If the horse behaves and goes along normally, the gumline has no effect; but if he tries to buck, inevitably he has to put his head down, and as he does so the gumline comes into action, giving him a short, sharp shock. The beauty of this device is that the horse inflicts immediate punishment on himself for making the decision to buck.

It is perhaps significant that the problems of one of the most experienced buckers which Max has had to deal with also originated in

ELIMINATE ALL POSSIBLE CAUSES

The gumline should only be employed as a last resort, and by someone experienced in its use, once all the other possible causes of the horse bucking have been eliminated. For instance, when the problem is pain-related, the cause of the pain is addressed, and the horse reschooled; in this case a gumline may not be needed. The use of this device is definitely not a first line of attack. However, with some horses it may ultimately be the only option, particularly those which have had the problem for some years and for which bucking is an established practice. The same theory applies to the use of the 'soft rope' on the underbelly of rearers: try all the other possible solutions first before employing this device.

the breaking procedure: here was yet another horse which had never fully accepted the saddle and had therefore never fully accepted a rider, either. His experience had been that whenever he bucked he had got rid of his rider, but was promptly punished with whips, so making him even more afraid of being saddled and ridden. Thus the cause of his problem was that he was thoroughly scared of the saddle: he shook whenever he was approached with one, and the whole issue had made him so anti-human that it had taken him four days even to 'join up'. It also took some time for this horse to accept the saddle, and so Max decided to employ the gumline before he actually got on it: he had to give it the choice of misbehaving so that it could then decide for itself whether or not to pursue the habit which had become such an established part of its life.

A powerfully built Thoroughbred, the gelding pitted himself against the gumline for a record three attempts, each time giving himself a considerable jolt when he tried to buck. He then threw himself forwards and walked on, and Max immediately patted him and then dismounted – this was the horse's reward for making the correct decision. Subsequently he showed no inclination to buck, either, even when given the opportunity to misbehave. He had learnt his lesson well, and now the horse that no one could stay on is being hunted and point-to-pointed successfully by his lady rider.

Teaching a Horse not to Pull

Many people over-horse themselves and find that they end up being out of control. However, some horses do pull your arms out and others will bolt. The remedy for both is to send the horse forwards, and to make it go forwards even when it is tired and wants to stop.

Coping with a known bolter does require you to be in a suitable place, somewhere such as a gallop where you can let the horse bolt and moreover insist that he goes further than he wants to. Do this, and then take him back the next day and make him gallop again, even if he is stiff from the previous day. What you are doing is setting up a situation in which the horse can realise that if he makes the 'wrong' decision – that is, to bolt – then life will become unpleasant because he will have to go further, and for longer, than he wants to. However, if he chooses not to bolt, then life will be comfortable.

A horse which was a known puller was sent to Max, who set up the situation so that he had the space to send it on. He rode with a completely loose rein so it had nothing to pull against, and kept it going by hitting its sides alternately with a piece of soft rope. If the horse wants to pull and gallop, then let it – but let it overdose on its pleasure and it will soon become so sick of pulling and galloping that it will start to say 'No thanks, I don't want to gallop any more'. It is rather like us having a feast of rich food: after a few days you just long for something simple and plain.

A Solution to Running Backwards

Persistently going backwards is a disturbing habit for riders. We were sent a filly which would do this, and dealt with it in the following way: after a certain amount of work she was happy to go forwards from the leg when in an indoor school – but out in the open she was still unpredictable. So she would be ridden out of the school and then made to go backwards for half a mile along the roadway; and at first even this was not enough to make her think and move forwards, so the backing continued for a mile and a half to the village. Travelling backwards is more stressful for the horse, both mentally and physically, and after a period of this treatment the filly was raring to go forwards: she chose to behave, and to answer the rider's leg by moving forwards, because this situation was much more comfortable than being made to back everywhere.

Quietly Does It...

How many times have you seen people waving their arms and shouting at horses, or prodding them with brooms or whips if they refuse to go somewhere, for example into a stable or a lorry? Unfortunately this is an all-too-common sight, yet the people who behave like this are only making matters worse.

We had a coloured pony which was none too keen to go into its stable; in the past something must have happened to it whilst it was confined in a stable to have instigated this worried attitude. The solution was simply to wait quietly until it stepped forwards, to the extent that after five minutes' deliberation, it would happily go in.

A mare kept in a low-ceilinged stable began to exhibit a similar fear of stables and buildings with narrow entrances. Because the stable was too low for her she had become headshy, as she kept hitting her head on a low beam. Naturally she also became unwilling to go into the stable – but was 'encouraged' to do so by handlers using whips. As a result she would always rush in and out. It was only when her final owner took the trouble to build a relationship with her and let her wait until she was ready to enter, that she learned to move in and out of stables happily and slowly. Interestingly enough the presence of one particular person who was always noisy and aggressive was enough to upset the mare and send her flying into her stable from a distance of several feet!

In a large establishment where many people handle the horses, it is quite possible that one may be led in or out of its box incorrectly and will bang its hips. If this happens a few times it will understandably start to be reluctant to go in at all, a situation which often develops to rushing in and out.

In all these circumstances, using a control halter can exert some influence over the horse's flight instincts. The halter is useful for dealing with horses that rush or bolt out of their stables, for those

FEEDING CHECKLIST

Follow these sensible rules for feeding to ensure that the nutritional needs of your horse are met but not exceeded:

- Always feed plenty of bulk, for example hay, or haylage. A horse's digestive system cannot function properly unless it has a certain volume of fibre passing through it regularly. When you think about it, the horse's natural lifestyle is to wander over many acres, grazing for at least sixteen out of every twenty-four hours.
- Feed according to the work the horse has *done*. You must be realistic about this: therefore a horse which is hacking round the countryside with just the odd schooling or jumping session is not being worked hard, whereas one preparing for Badminton Horse Trials will be – although yet again, there are some exceptional animals which work hard but require relatively small amounts of feed. Do not give your horse large amounts of feed because you *plan* to take him to a competition in three days' time; feed for the work he has already done, not what he *may* do in the future.
- Feed little and often in order to imitate the horse's natural feeding habits, and try not to leave him for long periods without feed; if he is left with nothing to eat for more than five or six hours his digestive system starts to break down. Stabled horses should have their 'meals' split into as many as it is practically possible to administer, allowing no more than five hours between each; the largest feed and heaviest haynet should be given at the end of the day, to keep the horse well supplied throughout the night.
- When compiling a ration, take into account the horse's age, breed, condition and temperament. Some breeds are very good doers – such as Britain's native ponies – and can look good on very little food; evolution has made them like this, and if, for instance, they are allowed access to extremely rich pasture, problems such as laminitis will result. Young horses have specific needs because of their growth processes, and older horses also have different dietary needs.

which barge or pull their handlers about, and for teaching a horse to accept being clipped. Of course this halter has to be used in conjunction with the psychological aspects of the work on the horse.

Feeding for Problems...

When horses were a part of everyone's lives there was a certain knowledge of how to look after them and feed them. However, as society has moved from its agricultural roots through industrialisation to our present situation, the links with horses have been weakened. Now these animals are kept primarily for pleasure, and the people who can afford to pursue such pleasures do not necessarily have a background in equine management. As a result, there is a great deal for these owners to learn, and one of the more complex areas is that of feeding.

There is a great deal of misunderstanding where feeding is concerned, and consequently considerable mistakes are being made which result in horses being fed incorrectly, often becoming 'over the top' in terms of their behaviour and posing real problems for inexperienced owners. For instance, one lady owner insists on feeding cubes intended for three-day event horses to her horse which hacks out for just an hour a day at the most; during the winter it gets even less exercise. She feeds event cubes because she likes to think that she is a part of that exciting scene – but then every time she rides she has a real handful of a horse. One day it will 'boil over' and the results could be horrendous.

Many of the problems a vet has to deal with have their origin in incorrect feeding; quite apart from the obvious ones such as azoturia or lymphangitis, wounds and even fractures may be sustained because the horse is too fresh and gets away from its handler or rider.

Any owner would do well to review his or her horse's feeding policy regularly – see the checklist for sensible feeding on the separate panels – and if in doubt, to consult one of the (free) feeding helplines run by feed companies. Many equestrian magazines offer a reader-reply service. Remember that sometimes it can take a while for the after-effects of over-feeding to work through a horse's system. For example, a showy, Thoroughbred-type pony we knew was extremely erratic in the show ring: although talented, it was very inconsistent, knocking down fences for no reason and being scared of its own shadow. Finally it was discovered that for years it had been fed a high energy diet, quite unsuitable for its type and for the sort of work it was doing; and although this diet was changed, for a while it still acted as if it was on the same high energy diet. Once that period was over, however, the pony went out and won classes.

Confidence: Its Vital Role

Confidence as a rider and owner is not always that simple to achieve. Moreover in just a few seconds confidence can be lost and it often takes a long while to regain it. Also, horses are very sensitive as to how positive their handlers are feeling: for example one horse we knew had belonged for about eight months to a very intelligent woman, and in that time seemed to have developed every possible disobedience: it bucked, reared, napped, pulled back, wouldn't tie up – it did everything that was bad! But after two weeks spent in our yard, it hadn't displayed any of its supposed problems, and was perfectly amenable to handle and to ride. So the owner was asked to come over, and a little later duly arrived and walked into the yard. The horse heard her footsteps, and after no more than fifteen minutes in her company, had demonstrated several of his bad habits.

It was obvious that the horse was an extremely dominant character in its relations with its owner: because she wasn't confident in the way she handled or rode it, it immediately took advantage of the situation. It was necessary to build up the confidence of the owner in order to help her towards a partnership with her horse; and what was particularly interesting about this case was how a horse's dominant attitude was obviously able to change if its situation and handler changed; and also the way in which association could play a part in its training. In this instance the footsteps of its owner prompted the horse to give a display of its dominance – although a horse's ready ability to learn by association can also be used to our advantage, rather than to its own.

FEEDING CHECKLIST

- The horse is usually fed 2.5 per cent of his bodyweight on a daily basis in order to maintain his condition. So for example if your horse weighs 1,000lb (450kg) his daily feed allowance will total 25lb (11kg). If, however, your horse is extremely fat, or obviously underweight, this general guideline will need to be adjusted accordingly. Thin horses must not be fed so much that they put on weight too quickly, as this will only stress their system even more; weight gain over a period of time is far more effective and preferable. The same principle applies to weight loss.
- Feed at the same times each day: horses like routine, and some may become stressed if their meals do not arrive punctually. They have an amazing in-built clock.
- If you need to change feedstuffs, do so over a period of time: this allows the bacteria in the gut to develop sufficiently to cope with the new feeds. Any sudden change of feed can result in colic.
- Always ensure the horse has access to fresh, clean water: water is vital for many of his daily functions and so is essential for life.
- Keep feed in vermin-proof bins, and ensure that all feed is used within the sell-by dates.
- Use only good quality feed; mouldy feeds should be disposed of safely.

Muzzling a horse to prevent him biting is certainly one option, but again, this young horse is not being allowed to make a conscious decision on whether to bite or not. If you are forced into a certain course of action you will be less committed to it than if you choose to do it of your own free will. There are probably many occasions when you have unwittingly 'backed your horse into a corner'; some may accept this and not react against you, but others will object, and if you do not understand why they are objecting, you will not be able to address the real issue

A Change in Behaviour

Imagine a member of your family starting to act strangely – perhaps being uncharacteristically grouchy, or not wanting to have as much contact with you. If that happened you wouldn't just ignore him or her, you'd certainly ask questions and try to find out what was the trouble. So if a horse starts to behave in a different way, shouldn't you also stop and think? Wouldn't it be a good idea to get to the root cause of the difficulties at an early stage, rather than just gloss over the warning signs and end up with a serious problem?

Millie was a good example of a horse whose behaviour changed due to a problem. Originally the Irish Draught x Thoroughbred mare had an enthusiastic rider who took her to many competitive activities. However, at the age of five she started to show signs that something was amiss, and quickly changed from being thoroughly amenable to behaving so badly that she was unridden for nearly two years. She was passed from pillar to post – she had been so honest, no one could really believe that she could be so bad; yet she would rear, buck and plunge and was virtually unstoppable. And the cause of all this heartache? The mare's neck was badly out of alignment, and she had a hook in her mouth – even though she had already been seen by a dentist *and a* 'back' man, neither of whom found the source of the problem. The hook was on the lower jaw at the back and was very large, and inevitably caused the mare terrible pain as soon as she was asked to flex, or when any pressure was put on the bit. Naturally she ran away from the pain – although if the rider dropped the reins then she would stop; but if he pulled back, then the mare got worse.

Eventually her problems were resolved; but she learned that she could still misbehave with certain people and get away with it – that she could change peoples' attitude towards her by the way she behaved.

Loading Horses: Tips and Solutions

This is a common problem, and one where it is difficult to achieve long-lasting results. All too often horses are faced with a situation that does worry and frighten them – but when they tell us they are confused and upset and just need a bit of time to 'tune in' to what is happening, we then abuse them, and try to force them. Joined-up horses are more likely to try things more readily, but if a horse already has a loading problem then sometimes just joining up is not enough for him to do things readily for you. But getting up behind him and trying to make him go forwards is no way to tackle the problem, and just gets his mind in reverse. Max uses the control halter – 'I need to get the horse freed up and coming towards me' – but the essential requirement is patience: you may have to stand on the ramp for hours and wait for the horse to come – but when it *does,* it will load itself on every occasion in the future.

Taking time is an investment for life – and you will probably find you don't need all the time you set aside for persuading the horse to go in. Your commitment to the horse should be that it is not going to have to fight. It is important therefore to work out how to present the situation so that the horse is comfortable with it, and to allocate enough time to achieve the objective – and once the horse takes that first step, the job is done.

It is far better to wait until you can devote the whole day to getting your horse on the lorry, even if it means you wait for weeks. If you try to do something too quickly, it is all too easy to get to the point where tempers start to get strained; and if you are tempted to hit the horse then this is a bad situation.

Being able to differentiate between the horse that is really thinking about what you are asking him, and the pony that is 'having you on' is also quite an art; some animals can swing from terrified, to ignorant, to cheeky very quickly.

Claustrophobia can play a part, and if it does then it may certainly dictate the way the horse behaves. Many people find that the horse will walk happily into the trailer, but when the ramp is shut and they move off it goes mad; or perhaps it goes into the box and then goes mad when the ramp is put up. This reaction is in fact purely instinctive: horses are not cave dwellers, and if they are worried about being shut

This horse was proving
unco-operative when it came
to loading

Max spent some time joining up
with the horse and then working it
in a control halter so that it
realised the situation was
uncomfortable when it resisted

in a trailer, or any other enclosed space, their natural instinct is to get out of the situation as quickly as possible.

How to overcome the natural reaction of horses like this is a real problem. One theory is to use ACP (acepromazine) tablets (a sedative available from vets) and then to load the horse, weaning it off the tablets over a period of time. However, the horse's adrenalin system is very powerful and can sometimes successfully challenge certain drugs; and then the horse may be so 'high' that it is difficult to re-establish its equanimity. The horse acting under the influence of adrenalin can channel its energies and 'close down' to anything else going on around it: it will concentrate on fighting against whatever it is to the exclusion of everything else. Thus using tranquillising drugs is not something Max agrees with: 'When a horse comes out of a comatose state he *may* be violent: if things go wrong – if the drug is unsuitable, or if the dose administered is insufficient – then the whole situation can turn out to be worse.'

Difficulties very often arise because of the way the horses are handled in the first place. Take the example of three ponies which live

However, when it stepped forwards, the situation was much more comfortable because the pressure from the halter disappeared

together: one of them is quite happy to load onto the trailer, but when expected to travel on its own, objects violently. As they do not want it to injure itself, the owners return home immediately, unload it and let it go back with its friends – and the pony therefore learns that by misbehaving it gets what it wants. What the owners *should* do is work through the problem, taking as many safety measures as possible (bandaging for protection, making sure there is nothing in the trailer which could hurt the pony).

A lack of understanding as to how the young horse explores a new situation can also cause people to behave in a way which does not help it. As an example, once he was halter-broken I wanted my young foal to learn to overcome his fear of going into a lorry. He was therefore allowed to sniff and paw at the ramp *in his own time*; next he put a foot on the ramp, took it off, put it on again, with *him* making the decisions as to when he performed these steps. And when eventually he did load himself he was *allowed* to lick and bite things: many people would have told him off for biting at the wood, but in doing so they would have denied him the chance of 'experiencing' for himself this new situation. Allowed a free rein in this respect he very quickly worked out that going into this large space was not as alarming as he had obviously anticipated. Thus he was invited to go along with his human friend and enjoy a new experience, he made the decision to go himself, and he was not hurt or frightened by anything. So the next time he was invited to go into a lorry he was quite happy to walk up the ramp, and he has been excellent to load and travel ever since, even on his own.

There are many reasons for horses refusing to go into the trailer or horsebox: maybe they lack confidence, or they have had a previous bad loading or travelling experience, or suffer from claustrophobia, or because for them, travelling is associated with bad memories, for example going to shows and being abused. Traditional ways of dealing with a bad loader include such measures as crossing two lunge lines behind its quarters, or whacking it with a whip or broom. However, if a horse is genuinely frightened, then forcing it in this way will only reaffirm its fears and it will undoubtedly be doubly reluctant on the next occasion. Certainly some horses do need lunge lines, in which case you must always be sure that you carry the relevant gear with you.

Another horse we knew was clearly terrified of the trailer, so Max used his control halter and managed to join up with it to some degree. 'He was evidently worried, but I got him to the point where he felt comfortable about being loaded into the trailer and the ramp being raised behind him. We then drove around the paddock at a snail's pace, and it was immediately clear that he didn't like his hips touching the side of the trailer – as soon as it moved he sank to the ground. So I then put my special "stall" rug on him and he was fine. Subsequently the owner fitted massive hip pads inside the trailer, and the horse has been perfectly confident about travelling ever since.'

The stall rug is a padded rug which Monty Roberts developed after he realised why so many racehorses dislike being in the starting stalls: the problem is that the stalls have ridges which dig into the horses' sides – and because horses are interpressure animals, they lean on them. With the stall rug on, however, they cannot feel these ridges and so do not lean into them, but stand up straight.

Never underestimate a horse's mind: it is amazing what some can work out. One horse refused to be loaded because it didn't like coming *off* the trailer; on one occasion it had panicked, leapt over the ramp and landed awkwardly, scaring itself. It was a front-unload trailer, and the solution was to make sure the horse felt comfortable about being loaded, but then to allow him to *back* down the ramp in order to come out. When he realised that this was the way he would be allowed to do things in future, he loaded straightaway each time.

It is not unknown for horses to be in a road accident, whilst in a trailer, and then to allow themselves to be re-loaded into a horsebox or trailer without any apparent apprehension. Do not be fooled into thinking that the horse must therefore be unaffected by its experience, however, because its reaction may simply be delayed. We knew one horse which turned out to be really deeply upset. Although he loaded initially, he increasingly showed his distress, his fear eventually culminating in him putting his legs through the trailer side and his head through the roof.

If a horse does suddenly start to be wary about loading or travelling, then search your soul for the cause of the problem: it may be only a small incident or mistake on your part, but your horse might consider it to be a major obstacle.

The Soft Touch and its Problems

For six years a dressage horse suffered pain because his neck vertebrae were out of alignment; but in spite of this, he was sufficiently talented to reach Medium level in affiliated competition. Owing to this pain, however, the horse had an attitude problem, and every time he grumbled about doing something his owner gave in to him and didn't make him do it. In time, the combination of pain and his owner giving in to him resulted in a horse which resolutely refused to submit to his rider. His evasions were legion: he would tolerate something for a few days, but would then retaliate with another set of tricks. After all, he had been allowed to say 'I don't want to do that' and get away with it for quite some time. It took months to encourage this horse back onto the right track, and the moral of the story is this: when something goes wrong it is important to address the hiccup straightaway, because if you do not, it will take much longer to achieve your objective. Think about why the problem has arisen in the first place, and if your first solution does not work, stop and rethink your plan of action.

SUMMARY

- The horse's flight instinct can be slowed down through the 'sacking-out' process: this desensitises the horse to sudden movements, touches or noises, and is extremely useful in many situations.

- When buying a horse be sure to take an experienced and knowledgeable adviser with you, try the animal thoroughly, and also have it vetted. There are unscrupulous people about who will dope a horse when it is being tried by prospective purchasers.

- Do not let your heart rule your head when buying a horse.

- Buy in haste – repent at leisure.

- Remember – let the buyer beware! Some people will go to extraordinary lengths to sell totally unsuitable horses!

Pawing to investigate is natural behaviour, so if your youngster paws at your trailer or lorry ramp when you are loading him, do not tell him off but let him indulge in what is natural; by pawing the ramp he is reassuring himself that there is nothing to be worried about

- Some horses are very dominant with humans, and fully prepared to take control all the time.

- A horse which knows he has power over people will be very tough to deal with.

- A horse which combines mental strength with physical power is indeed a force to be reckoned with.

- You cannot con a horse with acts of bravado: he will always know what you are really feeling. You will sometimes see people trying to 'brave' it out – shouting at their horses, hitting them, jabbing them in the mouth – but this is only to cover up their own fears or inadequacies.

Another demonstration of the horse as an interpressure animal. As a larger proportion of the horse's weight is on the forehand it is often more difficult to pick up the youngster's forefeet

SUMMARY

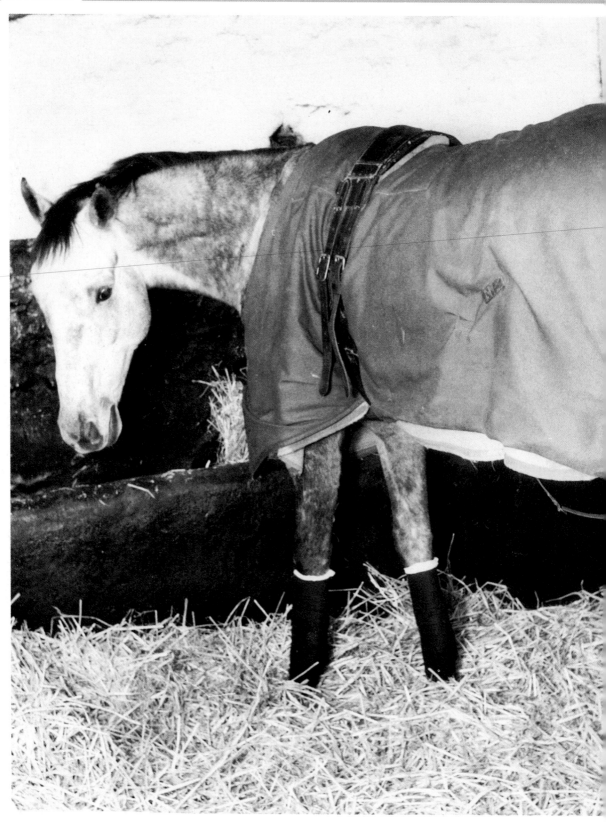

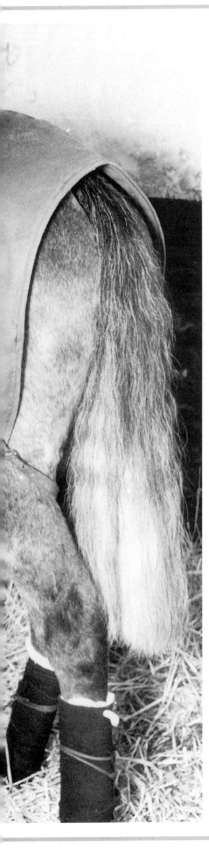

- Horse-owning is a major commitment: when all is going well it is just hard work – when there are problems it can be an extremely draining and stressful time; but if you take a horse on, then you have a responsibility to do the best you can for him.

- When things go badly wrong in a horse's life he often needs to be taken right back to square one in order to establish, or re-establish, respect and trust with a human friend.

- Horses are interpressure animals: that is, they lean into pressure. It is not, therefore, a natural thing for them to move away from the pressure of our leg when we ride them.

- Once a horse has made a conscious decision to stop doing something – for example bucking or rearing – he rarely goes back on his word.

- Horses learn through repetition – and if the repetition is of an unfortunate situation, then this is bad news for both the horse and its owner/handler/rider.

- We cannot teach the horse forcefully and expect long-lasting results, but we can set up the situation so he can learn for himself, and then he is likely to respond in the way we want for ever.

- Do not give way to frustration when dealing with horses, and never act in anger.

- Avoid over-horsing yourself.

- Ensure your stable management and handling techniques are good, and that they are based on sound reasoning (bearing in mind the horse's point of view).

- Horses are very sensitive and will react to your every different mood – so be aware of the messages you are sending out.

- If your horse's behaviour changes, ask yourself why.

- Invest time in your horse, and be committed to the result which is in his best interests.

- Take time to observe, think and learn about horses, because a part of the art of handling them successfully lies in being able to differentiate between those which are genuinely worried and are thinking things through, and those which are having you on.

- Adrenalin can take a horse over the edge of rational behaviour.

- Understand how a horse sees, explores and interprets the world.

Respect your horse's space and time; for example, leave him in peace to eat, rather than fiddling around with his rugs

IN CONCLUSION

The horse is a wonderful, generous creature, capable of giving great pleasure; it should not be thought of as a machine, or a status symbol, or the route to success in a particular sport. If you take the trouble to establish a real rapport with your horse you will be repaid many times over for the time and money you have invested in caring for it.

No matter how long you have been involved with horses, there is always something new to learn; this is why owning one is such a fascinating experience. And through this book, your increased understanding of equine behaviour should ensure that you have the most fulfilling journey possible with your horse.

Above all else, keep an open mind on all matters equestrian, ask questions, evaluate the answers – and listen to what the most important character in the scenario is telling you: ladies and gentlemen, the horse!

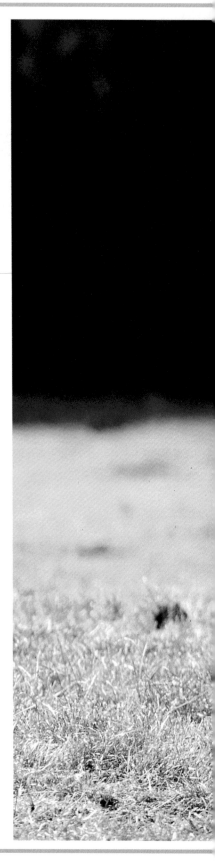

Getting a foal used to having his legs touched is good preparation for other things in life, such as having his feet picked out, visits from the farrier, having boots fitted and so on. Notice how the foal is exploring Max with his muzzle – he is not nipping or biting, and is allowed to smell, and touch Max without reprimand. The use of a longer-than-usual lead-rope also enables Max to work easily at the hindquarters. The foal is quite relaxed about all this

- Investing time in your horse means that you get to your ultimate aim more quickly.

- The methods as proposed in this book let the horse realise that if he wants to be bad he can be, but he will be so on his own. It is the horse which makes the conscious decision to submit to his handler and to behave well.

- Whilst genuine rogue horses are rare, each individual has his own temper and tolerance level, and this must be respected.

- Bad behaviour from a horse is usually an intelligent response based on its own survival instincts.

- Often a horse needs reassurance and understanding from its handler – but if we do not understand its psychology then we cannot appreciate when and how to help it.

- These methods rely on trust and a total lack of fear.

- If your horse is home-bred be careful that it doesn't become too familiar with you; remember that familiarity breeds contempt. Whilst you want a partnership with your horse, make it 51 per cent to you, otherwise some horses will railroad you!

- The horse has his personal space – and so do you, and neither of you should invade the other's unless invited to do so.

- When working with young horses you cannot expect everything to be in black and white; you have to allow for grey areas, and let youngsters be youngsters.

- Confidence is essential, and especially with young horses. If the handler or rider is too quiet and sympathetic this can make the horse nervous. He can sense the person's anxiety and this makes him unsure about what to expect next.

- The more you give young horses to think about the better, because bored animals may get cheeky. Constant stimulation of the right kind works in the handler's favour.

- You are not a bad person just because you snap at someone on an off day, so don't assume that a horse must be bad because he starts to misbehave. He may be in pain, or afraid or simply confused about what you are asking him to do.

- Don't become obsessed by your riding position: being confident and effective is far more beneficial to horses than looking pretty, but being ineffective.

Spend time with your horse in order to establish a lasting understanding with him, but remember that 'familiarity breeds contempt' – be sure that the balance is in your favour

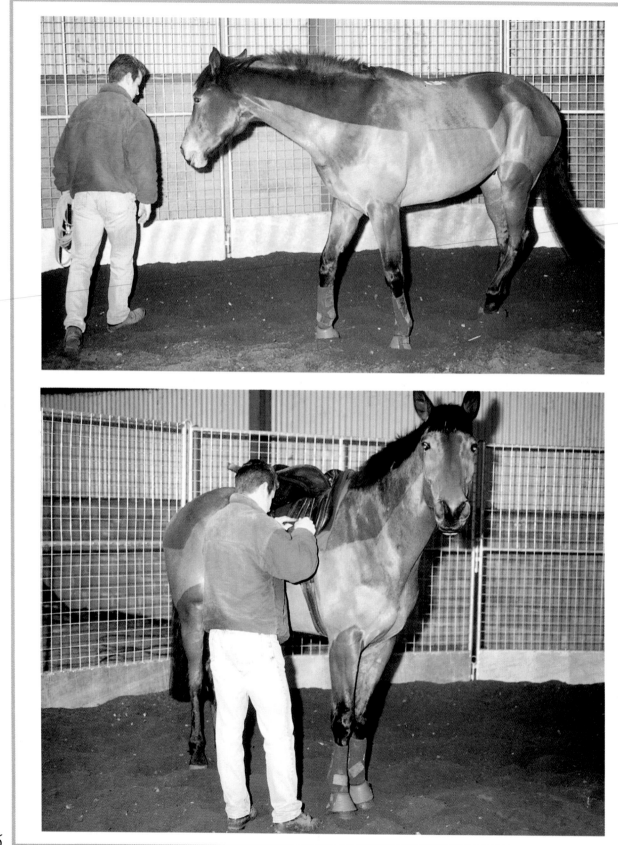

◀ *Before he starts to work on any horse, whether it has a problem or not, Max takes time to build up a relationship with it. This involves joining up with it, and in order to appreciate being with Max the horse also has to experience the isolation of being on the outer circle of the pen The horse has signalled that he'd like to be with Max – but his intentions are tested. If he is really serious he will stick with Max, twisting and turning to follow him. All horses find turning one way easier than the other: sometimes when asked to make a difficult turn the horse is not so committed to the partnership and is sent out to the outer circle again to reconsider his position. Full commitment is needed from both parties if the join-up is to be complete*

◀ *Completely unrestrained, the horse lets Max tack him up. An important part of the horse's education then follows, because he is allowed to experience the saddle at liberty, to buck, twist, turn, fly around, do anything he wants to get rid of the object on his back. Max believes that if a horse is denied this opportunity when he is first started, then at some point in the future the lack of full acceptance of the saddle will manifest itself and a problem may occur*

- You cannot teach the horse: it is your responsibility to create an environment in which it can learn. Once it has made the conscious decision to behave in a particular way it will keep its 'word' – but if it is *forced* to do so it will never be 100 per cent committed.

- When working with horses you need to put ego and pride to one side.

- A foal has a mind like a sponge, so expose it to all kinds of beneficial experiences. A horse's mind is like a window: at birth it is wide open, but by the time it is three or four it is barely ajar. It therefore makes sense to get the information across when the window is open rather than trying to jam things in later.

- Look at your horse and consider its breeding, and if it doesn't really look as it should, think about why. Could pain be affecting the way it moves and the way the musculature is built up?

- Don't just blunder along with your horse: think about what you are doing. The horse has millions of years of evolution behind it which affects its behaviour now and tomorrow.

- It is normal for horses to explore with their teeth: their muzzles are as sensitive as our fingers so they can be very gregarious with their mouths.

- Some horses are 'stable proud', and for them, being punished in their home is psychologically far worse than being punished away from it. It's like us being attacked in our home: it is 'better' to be mugged on the street, because then your home will still feel safe.

- If you have to chastise a horse that bites you, push and bump him because this is the way he is familiar with (horses tell each other off like this) rather than by slapping him.

- By confining a horse to a stable you may be giving yourself problems. For instance in a field a horse can avoid humans so he has no need to kick out at them. If confined in a stable, however, his flight options are non-existent, and if he feels the need to resort to close hand-to-hand combat then he will, by kicking or biting.

- A horse is a horse, not a human; yet some people expect a great deal from their horses. Remember that you need a balanced life: your horse is not there to fill a gap, for instance to be your 'child'. However, this does not mean that you should stop bestowing love on your horse – just remember that he *is* a horse, and treat him like one.

- Watch how horses discipline each other: they have stand-off points and shy away from physical conflict.

- Think about how you present yourself to your horse before you ask him to do things – otherwise you may take longer to achieve your aims.

- The horse's instinct when in difficulty is to revert to interpressure: they do not instinctively move away from the leg, and this is something we have to let them learn, by putting them in a good learning environment where they will make the correct choice, for example to go forwards from the rider's leg rather than to back off it.

- Stronger-minded horses are generally stronger physically, and even meek ponies can find the inner strength to run all over you; both horses and ponies generally have the mental backup if they are physically strong.

- Older horses that have been mentally and physically abused by humans take longer to be convinced that they *can* come to you, their 'new' human, and that everything will be all right.

- We may all have unwittingly abused our horses: for instance, a rider may have made a few mistakes, not meaning to hurt the horse but nevertheless in the horse's mind it *is* abuse – for example, getting its legs tied up in lunge reins.

- Beware of succumbing to frustration, when through sheer irritation you yank a horse in the mouth or give it one whack too many. In fact you are only making matters worse for yourself, because after you have given in to frustration you feel worse for being so weak; besides which you will have set your horse's training back several steps.

- If you are training a horse, then his progress is your responsibility, and only you are to blame if things go wrong: it is not the horse's fault, or that of his sire or dam, or any other equine relation. Humans are supposed to have superior intelligence to horses, and if we cannot control our tempers or think of alternative solutions to problems, then we should not inflict ourselves upon the horse.

- Never progress more quickly than the horse allows. If you do rush any stage of its education then at some point in the future your haste will come back to haunt you.

- Every individual is different and should be treated as such. As an example, Max recently started three young horses during a demonstration evening: the first horse took thirty-five minutes to join up with him, accepting the saddle and a rider; the second took twenty-seven minutes, and the third, an extremely laid-back animal, eighteen minutes.

- Good horsemanship is good horsemanship, whether it is seen as being 'conventional' or 'alternative'; the crucial factor is that you are getting the horse on your side and inviting him into the situation, and thereby providing him with an environment in which he wants to learn.

Trying to pit your strength against a horse is useless. As horses are interpressure animals they will lean into you – so if you want your horse to move back, there is no point in pushing against him

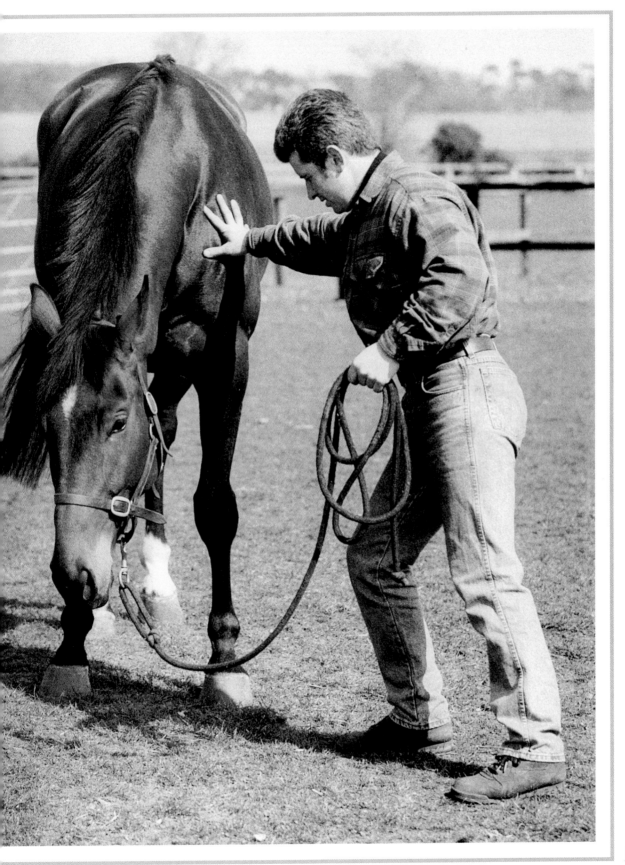

- We learn through relationships and experience, but we often deny our horses this opportunity.

- Don't confine yourself to the equestrian literature of your own country or your own time: there is much to learn from past masters such as Xenophon.

- The horse has a very simple, basic vocabulary: 'I submit'; 'I'm aggressive'; and 'I want to be with you and I do not fear attack from you.'

- Horses are like a riddle, and it is up to us to make sense of them. The language is there for us to understand, we just need to learn how – and it is something that we *can* all learn. There was a man who started horses using the methods described in this book, the difference being that he was blind. He attached a bell to the horse's neck, but he must have been so tuned in to that horse; how intuitive can you get?

Young horses need the company of their own kind in order to learn how to behave within equine society. However, their lives will be intertwined with human society so just leaving them to their own devices for four years and then expecting them to come into our world and become a riding animal is a tall order. Prepare your horse for his job in life by regular handling

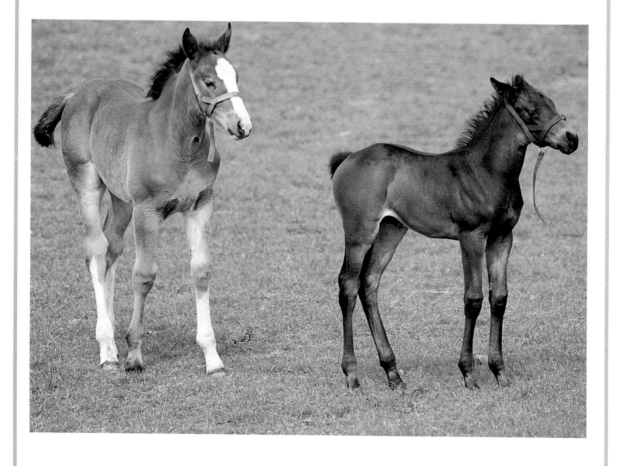

INDEX